GLOBETROTTER

Travel

PROVENCE
AND THE CÔTE D'AZUR

CAROLINE KOUBÉ

NEW
HOLLAND

★★★ Highly recommended
★★ Recommended
★ See if you can

First edition published in 2002
by New Holland Publishers (UK) Ltd
London • Cape Town • Sydney • Auckland

10 9 8 7 6 5 4 3 2 1

Garfield House, 86 Edgware Road
London W2 2EA
United Kingdom

80 McKenzie Street
Cape Town 8001
South Africa

14 Aquatic Drive
Frenchs Forest, NSW 2086
Australia

218 Lake Road
Northcote, Auckland
New Zealand

Distributed in the USA by
The Globe Pequot Press
Connecticut

Copyright © 2002 in text: Caroline Koubé
Copyright © 2002 in maps:
Globetrotter Travel Maps
Copyright © 2002 in photographs:
Individual photographers as credited (right).
Copyright © 2002 New Holland Publishers (UK) Ltd

ISBN 1 85974 840 6

Publishing Manager: John Loubser
Managing Editor: Thea Grobbelaar
DTP Cartographic Manager: Genené Hart

Editor: Tarryn Berry
Design and DTP: Lellyn Creamer
Cartographer: Nicole Engeler
Verifier: Elaine Fick
Picture Researcher: Colleen Abrahams
Consultant: Richard Sale
Proofreader: Claudia dos Santos
Indexer: Melany McCallum

Reproduction by Hirt & Carter (Pty) Ltd, Cape Town
Printed and bound in Hong Kong by Sing Cheong
Printing Co. Ltd.

Acknowledgements:
The author would like to thank the following
people for their assistance in the preparation of
this book: Richard Sadi for his knowledge and
company, Sara Louise Harper for her help with the
historical background, and all the tourist offices
throughout the region for their kind assistance.

Photographic Credits:
Mark Azavedo Photo Library/Chris Hellier : pages
7, 13, 14, 15, 21, 22, 24, 28, 30, 33, 34, 46, 56, 60, 71,
72, 75, 77, 78, 86, 90, 101, 104, 107b, 111, 116, 118;
Mark Azavedo Photo Library/Paul Shawcross :
pages 89, 93;
Sylvia Cordaiy Photo Library/Gable: cover,
pages 49, 58;
Sylvia Cordaiy Photo Library/Chris Parker: page 83;
Sylvia Cordaiy Photo Library/Jill Swainson:
page 6;
Sylvia Cordaiy Photo Library/Cees van Leeuwen:
page 55;
Image-Link: title page, pages 10, 11, 12, 16, 18, 25,
26, 27, 35, 36, 39, 40, 42, 44, 45, 47, 57, 61, 62, 64, 65,
68, 73, 87, 92, 94, 95, 98, 107a, 108, 109, 117;
PhotoBank/Adrian Baker: pages 52, 59, 99;
PhotoBank/Peter Baker: pages 37, 97, 114, 115;
Picture Works: page 9;
Richard Sale: pages 8, 19, 20, 29, 41, 74, 76, 85, 100,
110, 113, 119;
Neil Setchfield: pages 23, 80;
Robin Smith: page 4.

Cover: *The impressive arches of the Pont du Gard.*
Title Page: *Largely restored, old Nice attracts a
cosmopolitan crowd of visitors.*

CONTENTS

1
Introducing Provence and the Côte d'Azur

Two millennia ago, while the primitive tribes of northern Europe were waging battle with their neighbours, their southern peers were settling on the sunny shores of Mediterranean Gaul and building sophisticated towns to accommodate their victorious legionnaires and retired citizens. Die-straight roads, bridges, luxurious villas, theatres, arenas and pleasure baths were constructed for the new inhabitants so that they might feel as much at home there as they would have in Rome itself. Amazingly, much of what the Romans erected is there still.

The Provence of today is a heady mix of ancient history, solid traditions, and beautiful, often savage countryside; a landscape perfumed by its herbs and flowers, washed by a sensuous light and enriched, during those warm summer months, by music, opera and dance. It stretches its fingers out, ever languidly, to the rather more raucous and infinitely more flashy Côte d'Azur and the Riviera to its east.

The Côte d'Azur has largely pushed the past from its sights and created its own culture, one which gives precedence to the pursuits of pleasure. It is France's premier holiday destination, a meeting place for the rich and famous, and a coastal playground which still sets the standards throughout Europe. Yet, and this is its great trump card, behind the razzle of the Riviera, along winding roads that lead into spectacular hills, the gentler rhythms of life are still there to bathe the soul and feed the mind. What more could one want?

TOP ATTRACTIONS

*** Les Corniches: a spectacular drive along the Riviera.
*** Aix-en-Provence: a must during festival season.
*** Le Palais des Papes: situated in Avignon.
** Les Calanques: take a trip through these lovely inlets.
** Arles: Roman city, painted by Van Gogh.
** Gordes: a perfect perched village in the Luberon.
* Bouillabaisse dinner: in the Vieux-Port, Marseille.
* Horseriding: early morning through the Camargue.
* Saint-Tropez: fantastic for people watching.

Opposite: *Gardens, such as this one in Fontvieille, flourish in Provence.*

FACTS AND FIGURES

• **Area:** approximately 30,000km² (18,600 sq miles).
• **6 départements:** Alpes de Haute-Provence, Alpes Maritimes, Bouches-du-Rhône, Hautes-Alpes, Var and Vaucluse.
• **Main rivers:** Rhône and Durance.
• **Cities:** Marseille (1,230,000 inhabitants); Nice (342,000); Avignon (181,000); Aix-en-Provence (123,000); and Cannes (68,000).
• **Economy:** tourism, wine, agriculture and ceramics.

Opposite: *The impressive cliffs rising above the* calanque *of Port-Pin.* **Below:** *Views from Arvieux, in the Alpes de Haute-Provence.*

THE LAND

The area defined as Provence and the Côte d'Azur stretches across six French *départements* covering some 240km (150 miles) from the River Rhône in the west across to the Italian frontier, and some 160km (100 miles) from the northern boundary of the *département* of the Hautes-Alpes, right down to the Ile de Porquerolles, an island just south of Hyères.

Mountains

The majority of Provence is characterized by limestone hills and mountains, with the exception of the Rhône estuary. Two *départements* – Alpes de Haute-Provence and Hautes-Alpes – are regions of high mountains, alpine in aspect and rising to the region's highest peak, 3143m (10,500ft) at **Cime du Gélas**. In the central area of the Alpes de Haute-Provence, the heartland of Provence, **Mont Ventoux** is the highest point at 1909m (6260ft). Behind Monte-Carlo and Nice on the Riviera coast, the **pre-Alps** rise sharply from the shoreline and, although their summits are not much more than 1200m (3940ft), they are most impressive. Behind Aix-en-Provence, Cézanne's much-painted **Mont Sainte-Victoire** peaks at 1011m (3320m) and is a majestic sight even if, again, not particularly high.

Central Provence is crossed by a number of east-west hilly ranges. The Luberon is divided into the **Petit Luberon** with its flat-topped peaks and the higher, wilder **Grand Luberon** whose highest point is Mourre Nègre at 1125m (3690ft). In the south, the **Massif de la Sainte-Baume** (north of Toulon), the larger **Massif des Maures** (behind Le

Lavandou and Saint-Tropez) and le **Massif de l'Esterel** (behind Saint-Raphaël) are all striking ranges, the latter two forming a picturesque coastal backdrop.

Rivers

The River **Rhône** runs north to south into the Mediterranean Sea providing a broad fertile valley from an area north of Bollène and opening out to its flat alluvial plains south of Avignon. The **Durance** crosses Provence east to west, also providing broad alluvial valleys, but it has now been tamed by a series of dams that produce hydro-electric power. The **Verdon** rising in the northern Alps flows through the spectacular Gorges du Verdon.

Lakes and Lagoons

There are numerous small lakes in the alpine region of Provence. The largest is the turquoise-coloured **Lac de Sainte-Croix** and the long and narrow **Lac de Castillon**, south of Saint-André-les-Alpes. The largest lagoon area is the **Camargue**, the vast flatland delta of the Rhône (over 140,000ha or 540 sq miles) where the river splinters into myriad tributaries and man-made canals. It is one of Europe's prime wetland areas and a region of great ecological interest.

Coastline

Provence's coast is enchantingly varied. The sandy beaches of the Var near Saint-Tropez need little intro-duction, while the fjord-like inlets west of Cassis, the **calanques**, are simply spectacular. The smart beach resorts east of Antibes form the glittering **Riviera**. The Iles d'Hyères are much visited, as are the small islands – the Iles de Lérins – off Cannes.

CAMARGUE BULLS

The lagoons of France's Camargue are the domain of the Camargue bulls. Here the bull is king and he is followed in importance by the horse and, only then, man. Camargue cattle are gathered into *manades* (herds) bearing the owner's name, and handled by the *gardians* (cowboys) whose equestrian skills are equal if not more skilled than those of their north American brothers. The cattle are raised for fighting, breeding and for their meat. Camarguais traditions, such as the *brivade* (driving cattle to the *arènes*), the *bandade* (returning bulls to the fields) and *ferrade* (branding calves) are ritualized, and are times of festivity as well as work for the predominantly male *gardians*. Unlike bullfighting in the Spanish tradition, a Camargue bullfighter will not kill the bull. That is the role of a Spanish *toreador*, who adheres to a different set of rules.

Climate

With such varied topography, the climate of Provence is equally varied. On the coast the climate is typically Mediterranean: the summers are hot and largely dry with average day temperatures around 25°C (77°F), though some rain falls in the form of short, sharp summer thunderstorms. The winters are cool and average 12°C (54°F) as the cold continental air masses push southwards. The days may be rainy, though most of the rain falls between October and April, peaking in October and November. Away from the sea the climate is slightly more extreme. Aix-en-Provence often registers higher summer temperatures, but lower winter ones. The area around the Alps has pleasant, warm summers and cold winters. The abundant snow above the 1500m (5000ft) mark, ensures that this area is a favourite winter sport region.

Provence is also known for the **mistral**, a cold and dry wind which funnels down the Rhône valley, dropping temperatures a staggering 11°C (20°F) below the windless norm as it tears southward at speeds of up to 100kph (60mph). It forms when a high pressure area between the Alps and Pyrénées meets an area of low pressure over the northwest Mediterranean and can last for days at a time.

Vegetation and Wildlife

The vegetation of Provence has adapted to the predominant climatic tendencies by changing the size of its foliage so that moisture is not lost during the desiccating days of the mistral, or the searing heat of summer. It is here that the trees have thick bark and small leaves which, in some cases, are little more than a coat of thorns. Botanists find much of interest in the hilly and alpine areas: orchids, rhododendrons, gentians and Martagon lilies. There are cedar and chestnut forests at mid-levels,

---

PUBLIC HOLIDAYS

Jour de l'An, New Year's Day, 1 January
Pâques, Easter Sunday
Lundi de Pâques, Easter Monday
Ascension, Ascension Day, 6 weeks after Maundy Thursday
Pentecôte, Pentecost, 7 weeks after Easter
Fête du Travail, Labour Day, 1 May
Victoire '45, VE Day, 8 May
Quatorze juillet, Bastille Day, 14 July
L'Assumption, Assumption of the Virgin, 15 August
Toussaint, All Saints' Day, 1 November
Armistice 1918, Remembrance Day, 11 November
Noël, Christmas Day, 25 December

while the coastal areas have swathes of pines, as well as mimosa and eucalyptus. Provence is also known for its maquis, garrigue, cultivated lavender, vineyards, fragrant herbs and considerable fruit and vegetable cultivation.

The region's birdlife is prolific. Birds of prey are common in the mountain areas: **golden eagle**, **Bonelli's eagle**, **kite** and **buzzard** can all be spotted in the Parc National du Mercantour – one of the region's two national parks – while in the Camargue (much of which is preserved under the ruling of a huge *parc naturel*) it is the pink **flamingo** which graces both the skies and the lagoons. The Camargue is also known among ornithologists for the passage of migratory birds (such as the distinctive hoopoe, bee-eater and roller) travelling north in spring and south in autumn, and for its myriad duck, egrets, stilts and other waders, as well as marsh harriers.

This area is also renowned for its white horses and black bulls. Among the other creatures living in the Camargue are the beavers and coypu. In the mountain areas of Provence there are still chamois (though spotting them is difficult), marmots and moufflon, while boar and fox are found at lower levels.

Scuba divers enjoy the coastal waters and, in particular, the Ile de Port Cros where a fine variety of aquatic life can be discovered in the national park.

Opposite: *Nature lovers will appreciate the many different species of butterfly in the region, such as this Provence Chalk-hill Blue in the Mercantour National Park.*
Below: *The hazy mauve hues of lavender quilt much of the landscape of northern Provence during summer.*

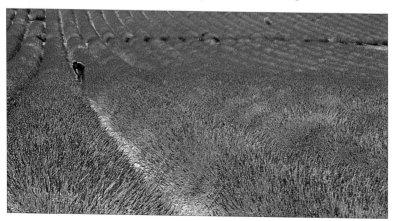

Below: *The egg-shaped
form of a* borie, *an ancient
stone house or shelter, is
often found rising above
the lavender fields in
northern Provence.*

HISTORY IN BRIEF

The immense **strategic value** of Provence, which is
bounded by the Mediterranean Sea and the River Rhône,
has resulted in a varied and violent history characterized
by constantly shifting boundaries, battling barons and
wave after wave of invasion. Celts, Greeks, Romans,
barbarians, Saracens, Catalans, popes and Protestants
have all contributed to Provence's tremendous **cultural
legacy** in various ways.

Early Settlers

Provence's ancient history predates the arrival of Homo
sapiens by an immense amount of time: caves in the
Alpes Maritimes and **Bouches-du-Rhône** sheltered
Stone-Age man nearly one million years ago. The first
proper settlements, evidence of which remains in the
form of drystone huts known as *bories* (*see* page 63), date
from around 3500BC.

From about 800BC a people known as the **Ligurians**
inhabited the region, building small fortified villages on
the hilltops. At around the same time the migratory **Celts**
(who were described as 'Gauls' by Greeks and Romans
because they reached Galatia in the Balkans) spread eastwards from Languedoc. **Ancient Greeks** from Phocæa
founded the colony of
Massalia (Marseille)
around 600BC.
Vines, **olive trees** and
pottery making were
introduced. Other
colonies were soon
established – the most
important being Olbia
(Hyères) and Nikaïa
(Nice) – and Massalia
became the hub of a
trading network that
extended throughout
France and the eastern
Mediterranean.

Under Roman Rule

Marseille supported Rome in its struggle against **Carthage** and in return Rome helped to protect Marseille against hostile neighbours. In 125BC Roman legionnaires saved Marseille from a **Celtic attack** then settled in the area themselves, creating a Roman province, known first as **Provincia** (hence

Provence) then **Gallia Narbonensis**, which stretched from Toulouse to Geneva and provided the springboard for the establishment of **Roman Gaul**. During the Roman civil wars Marseille backed the wrong side and was stripped of her independence and colonies by a victorious and vengeful Julius Cæsar in 49BC. Celtic-Ligurian resistance occurred intermittently until the final defeat by Augustus in 14BC.

Above: *Dominating the old town of Arles, its Roman amphitheatre is still frequently used for crowd-pulling events.*

The rationale of the Roman Empire was **conquest**, **pacification** and **exploitation**. However, the *Pax Romana* and a prolonged period of internal security transformed Provence's politics, administration, culture and economy. The Romans built a network of roads, and towns such as **Nîmes** and **Arles** underwent massive building projects, acquiring amphitheatres, temples, baths, aqueducts and the like. Roman colonists settled on the land, and large estates that dominated agricultural production were established.

Despite the legend that Christ's disciples – Mary Magdalene, Mary Salome and Mary Jacobea – landed in Provence in AD40, there is scant evidence of **Christianity** in this region before Emperor **Constantine** held a Church council at Arles in AD314. But when it did arrive it spread rapidly. Meanwhile, the Roman Empire, divided into east and west, suffered from a long period of anarchy and cultural and economic stagnation before the western part fell to the **Goths** in AD476.

THE FOUNDING OF MARSEILLE

According to legend, when Phocæan traders arrived in 600BC, their captain Protis attended a feast held in honour of the local chief's daughter, Gyptis. At the end of the meal the girl was allowed to present a cup of wine to the man she wanted to be her husband. She chose Protis and her dowry was the strip of land on which Marseille was founded.

Right: *Designed by Matisse, the simple yet stunning Chapel du Rosaire, in Vence.*
Opposite: *Dubbed 'Good' King René, this Count of Provence acceded to the throne in 1434.*

DIFFERENCES OF OPINION

Religious dissenters were fairly commonplace in Provence. During the 11th–13th centuries a sect known as the Albigensians (from Albi in Languedoc) were active in southern France and northern Italy. Obsessed with good and evil, and skeptical of much biblical doctrine, they were denounced as heretics by the Catholic Church. After the murder of the papal legate in 1208, the papacy and the French crown allied to launch the Albigensian Crusade, which brutally crushed the heretics. The last religious war in the area was the Camisard Insurrection in 1702–4, a revolt against government persecution during which Protestants in the Bas-Languedoc and Cévennes region sacked churches and killed priests. The government responded in time-honoured fashion with mass executions and burning villages.

Age of Anarchy

With the fall of the Roman Empire, stability and prosperity rapidly disintegrated. Barbarian forces from northern Europe – **Goths** and **Franks** – dominated Provence for several hundred years. Control of large areas and even individual cities passed from one power to another. **Saracens** (Arabs) made constant raids on the coastal towns in the 8th century and held the Massif des Maures and Saint-Tropez until 974, when they were expelled by **William the Liberator**, Count of Arles.

Medieval Provence

Provence became part of the Holy Roman Empire in 1032 but was still subject to **intermittent anarchy** and shifting local alliances. Individual cities (namely Arles, Avignon, Marseille, Grasse and Nice) asserted their independence and formed strategic alliances with other powers. The counts of Arles were superseded by the counts of Barcelona, who in turn faced territorial claims from the counts of Toulouse, the counts of Savoy, and the popes, among others. People withdrew to **hilltop towns** and villages, and settlements equipped with ramparts and forts (known as *villages perchés*). Several **castles** were built along the borders.

Provence became a major base for Christian warriors on their way to the **Crusades** in the Middle East (in 1248 the king of France, Louis IX, embarked on the Seventh

Crusade from the new port of **Aigues-Mortes**) and **trade** revived as a result. Romanesque **abbeys** and **churches** were built and **troubadours** toured Europe, singing songs in old Provençal (the *langue d'Oc*) of courtly love and political events. In the 13th century the Catalan Count **Raymond Berenger V** united the region under his rule. In 1246 his daughter and heiress Béatrice married **Charles of Anjou**, brother of the king of France, creating an **empire** that included southern Italy and parts of Greece. In 1308 the **Grimaldi** family from Genoa bought the estates of **Monaco**.

Papal Power

Avignon became the centre of the Roman Catholic world when the **pope** abandoned war-torn Italy in 1309. A **university** was founded and Avignon became a centre of **learning** and of the **arts**, extending its influence across the region. Clement VI purchased Avignon outright in 1348. Along with the Comtat Venaissin (west Vaucluse – granted to the papacy in 1271), it remained papal property until 1791. In 1377 Gregory XI returned to Rome but the French cardinals elected their own pope, thus creating the **Great Schism** which lasted until 1417.

> ### LES VILLAGES PERCHÉS
>
> Life in medieval France was turbulent and the humble citizens sought refuge in villages constructed to deter attack. Thus, the *village perché*, or perched village, was born. These small settlements grew up on nigh inaccessible heights, often on the foundations of earlier strategic lookouts. They were fortified by strong ramparts and walls and afforded necessary panoramas of the surrounding countryside. Well over 150 villages have been categorized as *villages perchés*. Among the most famous are: Bonnieux, Éze, Gorbio, Gordes, Lacoste, Lucéram, Menèrbes, Saint-Paul-de-Vence, Tourettes-sur-Loup and Utelle.

Golden Age and Annexation by France

From 1434–80 'Good' King René presided over a period of peace and economic re-covery, establishing a glittering court in **Aix** where **arts** and **culture** flourished. After his death in 1480 Provence lost its independence and became part of France, although the **Parlement de Provence**, based in Aix, retained a degree of autonomy.

The history of Provence from this point is inextricably linked with that of France. In the 1520s and 30s Provence suffered repeated **invasions** from the Holy Roman Emperor **Charles V** as part of his general campaign against France. **French** became the official language in 1539.

Wars of Religion

In the 16th century **Protestantism** spread throughout the
region and numerous abbeys and churches were ran-
sacked. In 1545 François I sent in the troops, targeting the
Vaudois (or Waldensians) in the Luberon mountains,
pre-Reformation heretics who had settled in Provence
long before its union with France. Three thousand were
massacred and 600 sent to the galleys.

For the rest of the century religious wars interspersed
with ineffective truces brought massacres and atrocities
on both sides. Aix and Marseille were centres of the
Catholic League, Nîmes and Orange were **Reformation**
strongholds. The **Edict of Nantes** in 1598 brought peace
by acknowledging **Huguenot** (Protestant) control of
certain areas. This posed a very serious threat to the
autonomy of the French crown by allowing Huguenots
to keep a number of fortified cities, which were effect-
ively outside royal control.

Kings and Cardinals

Seventeenth-century France was ruled by just two kings,
Louis XIII and **Louis XIV**, the Sun King, abetted by a
succession of able ministers, cardinals **Richelieu**,
Mazarin and **Colbert**, who were determined to concen-
trate absolute power in the hands of the monarch. To
strengthen the centralized state, key royal administrative

Below: *The small chapel
of Sainte-Sixte, near
Eygalières in the Alpilles.*

officials, the *intendants*, were appointed throughout the provinces and local laws were swept away. There was a gradual growth of **national identity** as opposed to regional alliances.

The **ports** of Toulon and Marseille were developed and the **textile** industry, especially **silk** production, expanded. But the 1685 revocation of the Edict of Nantes meant that thousands of Huguenots, to some extent the most productive citizens, left the south.

Above: *The traditional markets brim with locally produced pottery.*

Classical Provence

There is an abundance of good quality **clay** in Provence, resulting in a number of **ceramic centres** in the region. During the late 17th and 18th centuries the art of **faïence**, a technique of coating earthenware with a tin glaze, flourished. Louis XIV's **endless wars** had emptied the treasury, and the use of gold and silver dishes was banned. This gave a tremendous boost to the faïence industry, particularly in **Moustiers-Sainte-Marie** and **Marseille**. Agriculture and commerce prospered, and many of the great **mansions** in Aix and Marseille were built during this period.

Revolution and Aftermath

By the end of the century, a series of disastrous harvests exacerbated the ongoing economic crisis, which, coupled with social discontent, led to **revolution** and the end of the monarchy. In 1789 the Bastille in Paris was stormed and insurrections occurred throughout the country; Provençal peasants attacked local châteaux and monasteries. France was soon at war with most of the rest of Europe. The young **Napoleon Bonaparte** made his name by breaking the siege of Toulon in 1793; in 1799 he gained total control of France through a **coup d'état** and crowned himself **emperor** in 1804.

THE ROUTE NAPOLEON

Napoleon was forced to abdicate in 1814 and was sent into exile on the island of Elba. He staged a comeback when he landed at **Golfe-Juan** near Cannes the following year on 1 March with just over 1000 soldiers. From here he started his epic journey to Paris on what became known as the 'Route Napoleon', now the N85 running from the coast up to Grenoble, gathering support along the way.

Above: *The façade of the church of Saint-Trophime in Arles is noted for its exquisite medieval sculpture.*

Provence in the 19th Century

The Riviera was first made fashionable by holidaying English aristocrats who established **Nice** as a winter resort in the late 18th century. By the middle of the 19th century, improved **transport** – the development of railways and better roads, bridges across the Rhône and Durance and steamer traffic – enabled **artists** attracted by the luminescent quality of the light, and **foreign nobility** enticed by the mild winters, to arrive in force. Tiny fishing villages such as Menton, Juan-les-Pins and Saint-Jean-Cap-Ferrat grew into glamorous resorts, complete with opulent villas and grand hotels. **Monaco** boomed with the opening of its first casino in Monte-Carlo in 1865. Meanwhile rural life suffered a devastating blow when **phylloxera** ravaged the vineyards.

The 20th Century

The arrival of **American** artists and writers in the 1930s turned the resorts into year-round destinations. The introduction of **paid holidays** for French workers in 1936 and the cults of swimming and sunbathing caused the middle classes to head south and **mass tourism** was born.

Wartime Provence

After the fall of France in 1940, Provence lay within the collaborationist **Vichy government's** territory, then was occupied by German forces in November 1942 following the American landings in north Africa. Provence ceased to be a holiday haven and many towns were badly damaged. The **Resistance** (known as the *maquis* after the scrubland that made a good hiding place) was active in Provence, especially in the Vaucluse and in Marseille. Operation Dragoon was launched two months after D-day: on 15 August allied forces landed on the beaches of the Saint-Tropez peninsula and, with the support of the Resistance, were able to liberate most of Provence during the following two weeks.

THE BEAUTIFUL AND THE DAMNED

The writer F Scott Fitzgerald and his wife Zelda were just one of the glamorous expatriate couples who flocked to the playground of the south of France in the 1920s. Fitzgerald wrote his masterpiece, *The Great Gatsby*, while living on the Riviera in 1925. Hedonists and self-appointed representatives of the Jazz Age, Zelda declined into madness while Fitzgerald became an alcoholic.

HISTORICAL CALENDAR

1,0000,000BC earliest human presence in caves.
30,000BC Cosquer cave paintings.
3500BC early settlements.
800BC Ligurians and Celts arrive.
600BC Greeks found Massalia; first vineyards planted.
125BC Roman legions help defend Massalia.
118BC Roman Provincia is founded.
AD40 Mary Magdalene, Mary Salome and Mary Jacobea reputedly land in Provence.
AD314 Church council at Arles.
AD476 Western Roman Empire falls.
AD800 First wave of Saracen invasions.
1032 Provence becomes part of the Holy Roman Empire.

1096–99 First Crusade.
1246 Béatrice, heiress of Provence, marries Charles of Anjou.
1248 Louis IX embarks on Seventh Crusade from Aigues-Mortes.
1308 Grimaldi family buys Monaco.
1309 Pope Clement V sets up court in Avignon.
1377–1417 Pope returns to Rome; the Great Schism.
1481 Provence becomes part of France.
1545 Vaudois heretics exterminated in Luberon villages.
1598 Edict of Nantes proclaimed to end religious strife.
1685 Revocation of Edict of Nantes: thousands of Protestants flee south of France.

1720 Great Plague, Marseille.
1789 French Revolution.
1795 The *Marseillaise* becomes the national anthem.
1815 Napoleon lands at Golfe-Juan.
1854 Founding of the Félibrige, the Provençal cultural school.
1865 The opening of the casino in Monaco.
1904 Frédéric Mistral wins the Nobel Prize for literature.
1942 Nazis invade southern France.
1944 Liberation of Marseille.
1946 First Cannes Film Festival.
1956 Grace Kelly marries Prince Rainier III of Monaco.
1990 Mayor of Nice flees to Uruguay to avoid charges of corruption and tax arrears.

Postwar Era

The end of war brought **optimism** and **opulence** to the masses who came to the south of France in droves. At the same time the glitterati returned, and the **Cannes Film Festival** became an annual fixture for the rich and famous.

The region of **Provence-Côte d'Azur** comprising the five *départements* east of the Rhône was established in 1981. Provincial government has long been dogged by **corruption** scandals and the far right has reared its ugly head in Marseille, where outbreaks of racial tension and violence frequently occur.

In recent decades, waves of Parisians and British have bought up homes in **rural areas** but the Côte d'Azur remains the tourist magnet. Today less than 10 per cent of people work on the land and over-development, pollution, floods and forest fires have all affected the region's environment.

Below: *The tricolore of the French Republic.*

Below: *Arles' annual July festival sees some 2000 costumed Arlesiens.*

GOVERNMENT AND ECONOMY

Provence has always been considered the sleepy part of France where the climate hinders rather than helps labour, with the result that it used to contribute little to the economy. But as the coastal area became popular with well-heeled northern visitors wintering in sunnier climes, **tourism** began to fill the coffers in the 19th century. Large hotels and gracious villas were built along the attractive shore and gradually perceptions of the area metamorphosed. The Riviera and Provence are, today, among the country's most popular tourist destinations.

The Greeks introduced the vine and olive to France, the Romans refined their cultivation, and the popes, who planted **vineyards** in the 14th century, gave their wines a certain cachet. Devastated by **phylloxera** in the late 19th century, the vineyards were replanted with American cultivars. At the end of the 20th century, France was again replanting its southern vineyards with improved root stock and, thanks to better techniques, challenging the market for young wines from the New World with large quantities of quality wine. Provence produces most of France's high-quality **olive oil**. Also of high quality are the lavender essences, once a prime ingredient for the perfume industry and now more commonly used in enhancing household products or for aromatherapy.

Market gardening, and in particular the cultivation of *primeurs*, early fruit and vegetables, has also put Provence on the map. The region's stone fruit, strawberries, melons, potatoes, courgettes, aubergines and lettuce are exported throughout Europe. Although Provence is not exactly noted for its industry, it also has a reputation for glass, **ceramics** and pottery.

Monte-Carlo's revenues were once almost entirely accrued from gambling though the income from its casinos now only accounts for 4.3 per cent. The principality's income derives mainly from banking, real estate and business taxes, and the government is actively promoting the creation of **non-polluting industries**.

THE PEOPLE
Language

French is widely spoken in Provence though there is still some Provençal and one can find street names written in this old tongue. Provençal is the legacy of the *langue d'Oc*, once spoken throughout southern France. In the late 19th century the writer **Frédéric Mistral** was a leading light of the **Félibrige**, a group of writers who sought to re-establish the language. Mistral wrote two works in Provençal, *Mirèio* and *Calendau*, and from examples of the language compiled a dictionary and reference work still in use today. It is estimated that some 250,000 people speak Provençal, though most are over the age of 50. A certain nostalgia for Provençal ensures that it does not disappear entirely: it is still occasionally used for theatre. Other languages that can be heard in the market place include **Arabic**, for many are the immigrants in Provence who left Algeria, Morocco and Tunisia to settle in France, especially along the Mediterranean coast.

For the tourist whose French extends little beyond a *bonjour*, *merci* and *au revoir* there are few linguistic worries as the French, especially in the tourism industry, are quite capable of understanding English even if they are reluctant to speak it.

Religion

Catholicism is the most widespread religion in France though all the major religions are recognized here and their practices are freely tolerated. Other Christian faiths are also evident in the Midi: the considerable Russian community in Nice was offered the beautiful **Russian Orthodox Cathedral**, a landmark in the city, by Tsar Nicolas II. There are also various **Protestant** churches in cities where large communities of foreigners have taken up residence.

Above: *The onion-domed profile of Saint-Nicolas, Nice's Russian Orthodox cathedral.*

FAMOUS PEOPLE FROM THE MIDI

Nostradamus, (1503–66), astrologer, writer and doctor.
Paul Puget, (1620–94), architect.
Frédéric Mistral, (1830–1914), Nobel laureate, writer.
Paul Cézanne, (1839–1906), painter.
Alphonse Daudet, (1840–97), writer.
Marquis de Sade, (1740–1814), notorious libertine.
Émile Zola, (1840–1902), writer.
Zinedine Zidane, 'Zizou', (born 1972), football star.

Above: Santons *tradition-ally adorn Christmas cribs.*
Opposite: *A medieval Festival in Entrevaux.*

France's second religion is **Islam**. An increasing number of Muslim immigrants, especially along the Mediterranean coast, continues to expand the community. Marseille and Toulon are the two largest, both with important mosques.

Jews have lived in France since the 1st century AD, though they were forced to flee or convert when Good King René died in 1480. A further influx of Jews took place after World War II when many fled central Europe and, later, North Africa. The largest **Jewish community** exists in Nice but there are also synagogues in Marseille, Carpentras, Aix-en-Provence, Cavaillon and Isle-sur-la-Sorgue.

SANTONS

Small statuettes of saints (*santoùn*, in Provençal) made their debut in the late 18th century. During the period when churches were closed after the Revolution, a maker of religious statues in Marseille hit on the idea of making little figurines for creating **crèches** at home. They are fashioned out of clay into a variety of personages, fired in a kiln and painted in bright colours. The craft of making *santons* has been elevated to a veritable art. At the beginning of Advent each year, cathedrals, churches and homes throughout the region fashion a crèche and populate it with these delightful figurines. *Santons* have become collectors' items and in Christmas markets such as the **Marché de Noël** in Avignon, or the **Foire aux Santons** in Marseille, a large variety is on sale.

Festivals

Few festivals in Provence are of an entirely religious nature. In January, Monaco holds its annual **Festival International du Cirque**, a fascinating week-long event featuring the best circuses in the world. The **Nice Carnival** takes place in February, while Easter is celebrated with the first bull fights in **Arles**. May is the traditional month for the **Cannes Film Festival**, France's premier cinematic event. The end of May sees the colourful gypsy gathering at Saintes-Maries-de-la-Mer, with another smaller gathering in October. In June, La Ciotat hosts the annual **Festival of Cinema**. July kicks off with the **Feria d'Été** in Arles, with bullfights and parades, while the month-long **arts festival** in Avignon is one of France's major artistic events. In the same month, the country's best **jazz festival** takes place at Juan-les-Pins. Menton holds its **Festival de Musique** in August, and the **Lemon Festival** in February.

Marseille's **Foire Internationale** is in September, as is the **Fête des Vins** in Cassis, while Marseille's **Fiesta des Suds**, a music festival, is held in October. November sees Cannes's concert season and a **Festival International de Danse**. The best Christmas markets are the **Foire aux Santons** in Marseille and the **Marché de Noël** in Avignon.

The Arts

Provence's artistic legacy dates back to the Romans who colonized southern France and built some fine towns. **Arles**, **Nîmes**, **Vaison-la-Romaine** and **Glanum** are all examples of their expanding empire. The amphitheatres in the first two towns are still used for spectator sports, while the theatres at **Avignon** and **Orange** host annual theatrical festivals.

Romanesque Provence is vast. It witnessed one of the greatest eras of religious expansion and as the various orders managed to swell their coffers they built to the glory of God. The 11th-century Cistercians, who espoused humility and poverty, nevertheless bequeathed three magnificent abbeys and their adjacent monasteries. **Sénanque**, **Silvacane** and **Thoronet** should all be visited.

The beautiful sculpture which characterized much of Romanesque architecture can be admired in buildings such as **Saint-Trophime** in Arles, the **Ancienne Cathédrale de la Major** in Marseille, and the **Église Notre-Dame** at Sisteron.

Most of the medieval and Renaissance architecture is ecclesiastical but not necessarily boring. Look at Avignon's **Palais des Papes** – it comes straight out of a fairy tale; or the castles of **Beaucaire** and **Tarascon** standing opposite each on other either side of the Rhône, and the **Château Grimaldi** at Cagnes-sur-Mer. A perfect medieval town, **Aigues-Mortes** is well-preserved and a delight to visit.

Within the castles and churches are some fine art works. Among the artists to look out for are **Ludovic Bréa** who painted many beautiful altarpieces.

The majority of the region's villages and towns date from the period between the 13th and 16th centuries, if not earlier, and all have churches from this

DEDICATED TO THE MASTERS

A number of fine museums in the south of France are dedicated to renowned artists who lived and worked in the area. Among these look out for:
Musée Renoir, Cagnes-sur-Mer
Musée Matisse, Cimiez, Nice
Musée National Marc Chagall, Nice
Musée National Fernand Léger, Biot
Atelier Cézanne, Aix-en-Provence
Musée Jean Cocteau, Le Bastion, Menton
Musée Picasso, Antibes

Opposite: *Architect Charles Garnier designed Monte-Carlo's Casino.*
Below: *Ultramodern architecture for Arles' archaeological exhibits.*

epoch. Many of these villages are the so-called *villages perchés*, fortified villages often clinging to the summit of a mountain. What could be more memorable than a stroll through the picture postcard-perfect **Gordes**, **Éze**, **Saorge**, **Ramatuelle** or **Bonnieux**?

From the 17th and 18th centuries, Provence has few major monuments. It was a troubled time after the Great Plague of 1720 had decimated the urban coastal populations. However, there are still some fine buildings to visit in Marseille and Aix-en-Provence. Among those are the beautiful **Vieille Charité** by Pierre Puget and the **Hôtel de Montgrand** now housing the Musée Cantini, both in Marseille, as well as the **Pavillon de Vendôme** and the building housing the **Musée d'Histoire Naturelle** (also by Puget) in Aix.

When stability returned to France, building programmes for the wealthy accelerated and the *belle époque* was born. This was a great era for Nice and there are still many highly decorative buildings to remind us. Don't miss the hotels **Négresco**, **Carlton** and **Régina**, or the **Opera House** built by Charles Garnier as well as his gracious **Casino** in **Monte-Carlo**. Beautiful villas include the **Villa Kerylos** in Beaulieu and the **Musée Ephrussi de Rothschild** at **Saint-Jean-Cap-Ferrat**.

The last decades of the 19th and first part of the 20th century were a time of great artistic experimentation in architecture, painting and sculpture and saw some radical change in style. Towards the end of the 19th century the focus was on Paris where Impressionist works were drawing the crowds, but many artists were drawn to the southern coast for the exciting translucent quality of its light, the rich colours and the benign climate.

There are a number of museums along the Côte d'Azur and in Provence, which are dedicated to the canvases and sculpture of individual 19th- and 20th-century masters.

Dedicated to the work of **Pierre-Auguste Renoir** (1841–1919) is the Musée Renoir at Cagnes-sur-Mer; the house where **Paul Cézanne** (1839–1906) once lived in Aix-en-Provence has been preserved as the **Atelier Cézanne**.

Vincent Van Gogh

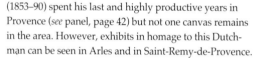

(1853–90) spent his last and highly productive years in Provence (*see* panel, page 42) but not one canvas remains in the area. However, exhibits in homage to this Dutchman can be seen in Arles and in Saint-Remy-de-Provence.

Artists who saw the transition from Impressionism through fauvism and into abstract art include pointillist **Paul Signac** (1863–1935), who spent time in Saint-Tropez, where a number of his works can be seen in the Musée de l'Annonciade, and **Henri Matisse** (1869–1954), to whom the Musée Matisse at Cimiez in Nice is dedicated. The Musée National Marc Chagall in Nice houses some 17 works by **Marc Chagall** (1887–1985), while the Musée National Fernand Léger has more than 348 works by the hand of **Fernand Léger** (1881–1955).

Jean Cocteau (1889–1963), intellectual, writer and artist, leaves a fine visual legacy in the Musée Jean Cocteau in Menton's Le Bastion. Works by the master, **Pablo Picasso** (1881–1935), can be seen in Vaullauris, Antibes and Mougins. The talented draftsman and painter **Raoul Dufy** (1877–1953) was similarly drawn to the Mediterranean and spent some years working around the Côte d'Azur. Work by Dufy is exhibited in the Musée des Beaux-Arts in Nice.

PICASSO IN THE SOUTH OF FRANCE

In 1946 Pablo Picasso (1881–1973) moved to the south of France, his main area of residence until his death. During these latter years of a long and productive life, his interest turned to **ceramics** and he spent time in Vallauris learning the techniques of this craft. Examples of his ceramic work can be seen in the **Musée National Picasso**, Vallauris, and in the **Musée Picasso** in Antibes.

A true-blooded Spaniard, Picasso was passionate about **bullfighting**, counting among his many friends a number of talented Spanish toreadors. He was often to be seen in the arenas at Nîmes, Arles, Fréjus or Vallauris. From his Mediterranean era, there are countless drawings and ceramic works illustrating his interpretation of the sport.

Other artists to take up residence in the south of France were Lithuanian émigré **Chaïm Soutine** (1893–1943), **Pierre Bonnard** (1867–1947), **Jean Dubuffet** (1901–85), **Hans Hartung** (1904–89), **Francis Picabia** (1879–1953), surrealist **Jean Arp** (1887–1966) and abstract painter **Nicolas de Staël** (1914–55).

The modern era in Provence has produced some interesting buildings designed mostly to house museum collections. In Nîmes the **Carrée d'Art**, a glass-and-steel confection by Briton, Norman Foster, is as elegant as the Roman temple it faces. Housing a modern collection, the **Musée d'Art Contemporain** in Nice deserves a moment, as does the building housing the **Fondation Mæght** in Vence. In this town, too, is Matisse's beautiful **Chapelle du Rosaire**, a gem of modern religious architecture. **Le Corbusier** was responsible for the design of Marseille's postwar **Cité Radieuse**.

An unusual, though highly successful project was the creation of **Port Grimaud** in the 1960s by François Spoerry. With the passage of a few decades, this well-conceived port has blended successfully into the landscape and become the inspiration for numerous marine projects worldwide.

LA CITÉ RADIEUSE

Brainchild of architect **Le Corbusier** (1887–1965), La Cité Radieuse in Marseille is the best known of five similar housing schemes designed by him. Following the formula known as the *Modulor*, where a given dimension equals the sum of the two previous dimensions, Le Corbusier created what he considered perfect apartment blocks: attractive, user-friendly homes. In Marseille this *Unité d'Habitation*, built between 1947and 1952, comprises **337 apartments** of 15 different types, each one with a terrace and pleasant view. Within the *cité* are indoor shops, a restaurant, a junior school and even an open-air theatre. If the project seems dated now, it was a forerunner at its unveiling. It has been declared a *Monument Historique* by the French government.

Music and Literature

The 14th-century poet laureate **Petrarch** was one of the earliest writers to evoke life in Provence (he lived out his love-sick life in Vaucluse). In the 16th century **Nostradamus** wrote his controversial work *The Centuries* in Salon-de-Provence, and the infamous 18th-century **Marquis de Sade** published *Justine* here, but Provence is more commonly associated with 19th- and 20th-century writers. The greatest of these was probably **Frédéric Mistral** (1830–1914), the respected poet laureate whose poem *Mirèio* is a classic in French literature. He did much to promote his native language, Provençal. **Alphonse Daudet**, who wrote *Letters from My Windmill*, lived near Fontvieille (you can visit his windmill).

The advent of cinema and musicals resulted in a number of productions that captured a little of the Provençal spirit which might otherwise have remained obscure to the rest of the world. These include adaptations of **Alexandre Dumas'** *The Count of Monte Cristo*, **Marcel Pagnol's** *Jean de Florette* and *Manon des Sources*, and **Victor Hugo's** *Les Miserables*.

In the heady days at the beginning of the 20th century, **American authors** such as Edith Wharton, F Scott Fitzgerald and Ernest Hemingway fell in love with the Côte d'Azur, while **English writers** like Graham Greene, Anthony Burgess and actor Dirk Bogarde (*A Postillion Struck by Lightning*) also succumbed to the region's beauty.

More recently, British advertising man turned writer, **Peter Mayle**, gained notoriety when he moved to the Luberon and wrote a frank account of life with his neighbours (*A Year in Provence*) followed by a number of equally successful novels.

Much as Provence was loved by artists, it seems not to have had much effect on **musicians**, and few made Provence their home. However, this lapse is more than compensated for nowadays and the region has become a showcase for modern French culture. Various annual festivals take place, especially during the summer. Traditional theatre and music are complemented by contemporary works and fringe events. **Avignon**, **Aix-en-Provence** and **Orange** are the prime venues for these festivals.

> ### THE FÉLIBRIGE AND FRÉDÉRIC MISTRAL
>
> The Félibrige was an intellectual movement founded in 1854 by seven young poets, dedicated to the revival of the Provençal language. Its most famous member and stalwart defender of Provençal regional identity and traditions was **Frédéric Mistral** (1830–1914), who won the Nobel Prize for literature in 1904. He set up an **ethnographic museum** in Arles with his prize money to depict every aspect of Provençal life, history and folklore.

Opposite: *A late portrait of Frédéric Mistral.*
Below: *The Inspiration for Daudet's* Letters from my Windmill.

Feeling peckish? The markets and backstreets are great for a little snack. Look out for *pissaladière*, pizza's French cousin; a slice of *pâte en croûte*, very tasty pâte-filled pastry; a strip of *fougasse*, flat-bread cousin to Italy's *foccaccia*. Fancy breads and rolls will often include local olives and raisins, but if you have a real sweet tooth, try the *calissons*, sweet biscuits sometimes filled with citrus peel or chocolate, and other delights sold by weight not quantity. For the gourmand, *pâtisseries* sell a delicious though not inexpensive range of light pastries filled with sweet cream and fresh fruit. They sell tarts by the slice too, as well as quiche and pizza. Thanks to the large Asian and African population, you'll also be able to find savoury *samosas* and *nems,* spring rolls, as well as take-away portions of couscous or paella.

Sport

There can hardly be a better area in France for sporting enthusiasts. **Winter sports** lovers take to the pistes in the Parc National du Mercantour at Isola 2000, the Val d'Allos, Annot-Allons (cross-country skiing) or the three resorts around Barcelonnette. **Hikers** will find myriad trails through the numerous natural and two national parks. France is well equipped for its *randonnés* (hiking trails). Not only are hiking maps easily available, but trails are well graded and marked.

Cyclists, too, are welcome – indeed, the **Tour de France** passes through Haute-Provence and leaves in its wake a passion for biking. Monte-Carlo hosts regular international **tennis** matches in springtime, and all over the region tennis is a popular pastime. Watersport fans can indulge in **canoeing** on Provençal rivers, through canyons such as those as Verdon or the Ardeche, around Antibes and through the Calanques near Cassis (a popular venue for **rock-climbers**, too), or tracing a course around islands such as the Iles d'Hyères. **Scuba divers** likewise head for the Iles d'Hyères, while **windsurfers** will be able to hire boards along most of the coast. **Swimmers** will find plenty of opportunity for a dip all along the Mediterranean from May to October. The lakes and rivers of Provence are also popular in the high summer. **Golfers** have the opportunity to tee off at some of the Riviera's excellent (though expensive) courses.

Right: *Canoeing is a popular pastime on the turquoise waters of Lac de Sainte-Croix.*

Perhaps the most famous spectator sport on the annual calendar is the **Grand Prix de Monaco**, held six weeks after Easter, when Formula I cars hurtle through the principality with alarming speed.

Bullfighting is a popular spectator sport in summer. Nîmes and Arles boast the most famous (Roman) amphitheatres where an afternoon or evening *corrida* will take place. Provence's own version, the *cocarde* (a group of young men against a bull who, hero or loser, leaves the ring alive), is also very popular, particularly in Arles.

And lastly, visitors to the Camargue will want to go **horseback riding** on those beautiful white steeds. There are many opportunities around Saintes-Maries-de-la-Mer.

Above: *Provence's olives are to be found in all markets, in a variety of forms and colours.*

Cuisine

Provence is the cradle of French cuisine and its kitchen garden. The region produces many of the country's **vegetables** and **fruits**. Seasoned with herbs or wild mushrooms and added to beef, lamb or regional seafood, they seal a perfect meal. Naturally, various crispy breads, baguettes or rolls, served with a local goat or cow's milk cheese and choice wine, accompany even the simplest of dishes.

Provence produces the country's luscious olives, its fine **olive oil**, and a large range of aromatic plants and herbs. Best of all, these ingredients are not the prerogative of locals only – they are available in the many colourful markets throughout Provence and the Côte d'Azur.

Provence is known for its fine tomato sauces, but it also makes *pistou* with garlic, basil and olive oil: the French answer to Italian pesto. This is used in soups like the traditional *soupe au pistou*, and as accompaniment to the lamb reared in the hills around Sisteron. *Tapenade*, an anchovy and olive paste often used as a dip, is also

---

THE VERSATILE OLIVE

We know that olive trees existed 6000 years ago, but it was only 4000 years later that man began extracting its oil for lubrication, soap and human consumption. Over 95 per cent of the world's olive oil is produced around the Mediterranean. France is ranked as a small but important producer, pressing oil for culinary purposes – Provençal cuisine is noted for its liberal use of this delicious and highly nutritious ingredient. Look out for the different categories: **extra virgin** with less than 1 per cent acidity, **virgin** with 1–2 per cent and **olive oil** (without the word 'virgin') with below 3.3 per cent acidity.

Above: *Early vegetables are Provence's great drawcard.*
Opposite: *The popes' vineyards at Châteauneuf popularized Rhône wines.*

often used to flavour sauces. Other sauces include *aïoli*, a garlic-flavoured mayonnaise frequently served with fish. Probably the most famous soupy dish is Marseille's *bouillabaisse*, produced with at least three fishes, eel, tomatoes, garlic and olive oil. The soup is served first, with *rouille* – a Provençal sauce made from eggs, garlic, olive oil and saffron – as well as toasted baguette and grated cheese. Then the fish is served, with yet more broth and potatoes.

Although the country's best beef is Charolais from Burgundy, **Camargue beef** is also highly rated. *Daube de bœuf*, beef braised in red wine, is a popular dish as is *agneau* (lamb), the finest of which comes from the Alps around Sisteron. Young duck (*canette*) is often served with sweet baby onions, or smoked. Chicken is less common on menus, though served in a Provençal sauce made of tomato, pepper and onion, it is very tasty.

Fish and **seafood** is ubiquitous on the coast. Lobster and prawns are expensive but popular items on the Côte d'Azur. Fish appears on all menus. *Loup*, *Saint-Pierre*, *dorade*, *baudrois* and sole are considered the best while, in season, tuna is popular. Fish is usually served grilled with an accompanying sauce, pan-fried with herbs or served in a stew such as *bouillabaisse*.

Les Primeurs, the first vegetables of the season (green beans, aubergines, courgettes, tomatoes, bell peppers and new potatoes), herald the summer and characterize the dishes of Provence and the Côte d'Azur. These popular vegetables characterize dishes such as *papeton d'aubergine*, an aubergine mousse served with fresh tomato sauce; courgettes are the basis of *ratatouille*, but they are also served stuffed with such delicacies as goat's-milk cheese, and even meats and fish *brandade*. The use of vegetables is rather low-key compared to

---

ANTOINE DE SAINT-EXUPÉRY (1900–1944)

Internationally renowned as the author of *The Little Prince*, a tale for both adults and children, Antoine de Saint-Exupéry was a French aviator who died on a recon-naissance expedition during World War II. He was lost at sea in 1944 in his own plane, a Lightning P38, and never found. In 1998, the captain of a Marseille fishing boat revealed that he had found an amulet in his nets just a few kilometres from the famous Cosquer Cave.
In 2000, local diver Luc Van Rell salvaged remains of a wartime aircraft from the waters. It is believed to be the wreckage of Saint-Exupéry's plane, but is still subject to definitive authentication.

the way the Anglo-Saxons serve them, but with a choice of salads, **vegetable terrines** and fresh fruit even vegetarians can manage well.

Cheese, of course, is *de rigeur* on the French dining table. In Provence the best cheeses come from the highland areas of Haute-Provence. *Chèvre* cheeses, produced from goat's milk, come in various forms, while *fromage de brebis*, made with ewes' milk, is a delectable alternative to the more common choice of cow's-milk cheeses.

Desserts in this part of France encompass a good range of local, seasonal fruits: figs, cherries, peaches, kiwi fruit, nectarines, strawberries, melons, raspberries, blackcurrants, apples and pears. You should also try sweet dishes such as *tarte au citron* (lemon tart), *feuilleté de fruits*, *mousse au citron* or *au chocolat*.

Aperitifs and Wines

Pastis is Provence's drink par excellence. This aniseed-flavoured alcoholic beverage is diluted with water and ice and consumed as a refreshing aperitif. Ask for Pernod or Ricard by name.

Provence has 16 AOC (*Appellation d'Origine Contrôlée*) regions where the quality and consistency of its wines are controlled and assured. Among these you'll drink **wines** from Châteauneuf-du-Pape, Côtes de Provence, Rosé de Tavel, Muscat de Beaumes-de-Venise, Côtes de Ventoux, Gigondas, Cassis or Bandol. With the exception of the *appellation* **Châteauneuf-du-Pape**, these wines are, arguably, not as fine as their competitors from Bordeaux or Burgundy, but have still succeeded in creating a name for themselves both regionally and nationally. The increasing pressure to sustain their industry against an onslaught of numerous cheaper wines from other sources has resulted in a finer Provençal product.

WINE THROUGH THE AGES

Almost half the cultivated land in Provence is under vines, with olives and almonds making up a substantial percentage of the rest. The ancient Greeks planted vines on the hills surrounding Massalia in the 6th century BC and the Romans produced wine that was fine enough to be exported to Rome. Climatic conditions are torrid due to the fierce southern sun, a serious shortage of rain and the effects of the mistral which blasts down the Rhône. Red wines perform best here and the southern Côtes du Rhône boasts some very prestigious names, such as Gigondas, Vacqueyras and Châteauneuf-du-Pape, whose first vineyards were planted in 1317 by Pope John XXII. The Côtes de Provence is known for its rosés, first promoted by King René in the mid-15th century.

2
Bouches-du-Rhône

The River Rhône finishes its long journey in the flatland area of the Camargue, where it splits into myriad sluggish channels and man-made canals that give the name Bouches-du-Rhône (mouths of the Rhône) to one of France's most interesting provinces. It is a fascinating area renowned for its wildlife, its beautiful provincial towns and Roman remains.

Marseille, the capital of Provence, started life as Massalia. It was a safe harbour built by the Greeks, thus making it the country's oldest port, and for nearly three millennia it has been used as a trading point in trans-Mediterranean commerce. Today it is a vibrant, large city which still derives much of its income from its port, but thanks to postwar rebuilding it is gradually shrugging off its tarnished image for one of a modern, cosmopolitan metropolis.

A string of attractive towns garland the centre of this *département*, all with the tag 'Provence' which gives them a certain cachet. **Aix-en-Provence**, a thriving university town and well-known festival venue, is one of France's prettiest towns. No one monument distinguishes it: Aix is a synthesis of all that is Provençal. Nearby, the gleaming white peaks of **Mont Sainte-Victoire** provided great inspiration for that much-loved Provençal artist, Paul Cézanne. **Les-Baux-de-Provence** takes its name from the impressive escarpments amid which the medieval settlement was constructed, and **Saint-Rémy-de-Provence**, a fashionable small town, is ideal for exploring the heartland of the region.

DON'T MISS

*** Les Calanques: near Cassis, fabulous sea inlets.
*** Arles: with its incredible Roman arena.
*** Aix-en-Provence: preferably at festival time.
** The Camargue: for its wilderness and wildlife.
** Les Alpilles: and the towns within the area.
** Mont Sainte-Victoire: beloved of Cézanne.
* Vieille Charité: Marseille.
* Bouillabaisse dinner: on Marseille harbour.

Opposite: *The huge arches of the Pont du Gard rise above the River Gardon near Nîmes.*

MARSEILLE

France's third largest and most ancient city, Marseille has a vibrant rhythm that embraces both sides of the Mediterranean. During its 2600-year history, Marseille has remained an important harbour, a trading post between Europe and Africa and a point of immigration for countless foreigners, many of whom have remained in the city adding their own distinctive cultures to the Mediterranean melting pot.

Marseille knew periods of depression such as the plagues in the 18th century which wiped out half its population, but during the 19th century the city rediscovered its importance, thanks in part to the building expansion under the Second Empire, and also because of the opening of the Suez Canal.

Le Vieux-Port ***

This is the focal point of old Marseille and the area around which most of the tourist sights are located. On either side of the deep, rectangular port – the city's prime mooring for yachts as well as cruisers – there are bustling restaurants lining the quays. Behind **Quai du Port** which terminates at the **Fort Saint-Jean**, the narrow streets and flights of steps ascend the hillside through **Le Panier** district, an area that was much damaged in World War II. Subsequent rebuilding has married modern architecture with older, surviving buildings. Here you'll find the grandiose **Hôtel de Ville**, known simply as the **Mairie**, a 17th-century work by Marseillais, Pierre Puget. Nearby, the **Maison Diamantée** – so called for the diamond shaped protrusions from its walls –

houses the **Musée du Vieux-Marseille** (at 2 rue de la Prison, open Wednesday to Monday) where you'll see a fascinating collection of folk art – paintings, *santons* (religious figurines used for nativity scenes), embroidery and costumes.

At the western extreme of the port, you can climb up to the **Église Saint-Laurent**, a 12th-century church that is gradually returning to its former splendour thanks to an excellent renovation programme. The views from the **place Saint-Laurent** are well worth the climb.

On the opposite, (southern) side of the port – linked by the **Quai des Belges** (the venue for the morning fish market) – the **Quai de Rive Neuve** terminates in the massive Fort Saint-Nicolas. Rising above the port is the **Basilique Saint-Victor**, with an exterior more fortress-like than a temple to religion. It was erected by Jean Cassein on the site of Saint Victor's martyrdom (AD304), subsequently enlarged with a monastery in the 12th century and reinforced in the 14th to give it the solid, yet simple Romanesque form that is seen today.

Above: *The Old Port and the well-proportioned Hôtel de Ville are situated in the heart of Marseille.*

The Cathedrals *

It is unusual to find two cathedrals side by side, but this is the case in Marseille. High above the crooked roads of the Panier Quarter of the city, you'll reach the **Ancienne Cathédrale de la Major**, the city's delightful, small and original 12th-century Romanesque building in which Catherine de Medici was married. **La Cathédrale de la Nouvelle Major**, by contrast, is large and highly visible. A neo-Gothic or Roman Byzantine building, it was constructed in the 19th century using some of the original stone from a former cathedral with the addition of new marble and porphyry.

BEST MARKETS

Aix: flower market, Tuesday, Thursday, Saturday.
Antibes: Cours Masséna, every morning, except Monday.
Cannes: Marché Forville, daily.
Carpentras: Friday mornings.
Marseille: Cours Julien, daily, except Monday, and Quai des Belges.
Nice: Cours Saleya, daily.
Toulon: every morning, except Monday.

Right: *The gracious lines of the Centre de La Vieille Charité, one of architect Pierre Puget's most successful projects.*

Centre de la Vieille Charité ★★★

Not far from the cathedrals, this magnificent 17th-century hospice (2 rue de la Charité, open daily, except Monday) was designed by Louis XIV's architect, Pierre Puget, and constructed to house the city's orphans and homeless fleeing war and famine. Today the fine chapel under its Baroque, elliptical dome offers exhibition space, and in the elegant arcaded surrounds the **Musée d'Archéologie Méditerranéene** is housed. On show here are pieces from most of the Mediterranean countries, with some excellent exhibits, in particular, from Egypt. Look at the small yet superb 4500-year-old statue of a youth from Giza, the serpentine mummy cases and the 2300-year-old sarcophagus in the form of an ibis. Lovers of African or Oceanic art will discover that the exhibits in the **Musée d'Arts Africain**, **Océanien et Amérindien** are most worthwhile.

Basilique de Notre-Dame-de-la-Garde ★

Standing 154m (505ft) above the city, the basilica has a privileged panorama of all Marseille and the islands offshore. It has been a sanctuary for nearly 800 years but the present building, finished in 1864 and topped by a golden statue of the Virgin, is not to everyone's taste. Its lopsided façade, tall tower, glittering mosaics and apses, and tall tower, are all executed in neo-Byzantine style. Even if that doesn't appeal one cannot fail to be moved by the breathtaking view.

Canebière Area **

Marseille's largest boulevard, a commercial axis from which you'll see the elegant **Bourse** (housing the **Musée de la Marine et de l'Économie**) and nearby, the Art Deco **Opéra** (rebuilt in 1924) and fashionable **rue Paradis**, this road was originally where the city's hemp was grown. As you stroll along, you'll cross the summer garlic sellers along **cours Belsunce** which ends to the north in the triumphal arc **Porte d'Aix**, and to the south in the **place Castellane**, with its distinctive column.

Walking up **rue Grignan**, a semi-pedestrian-only street filled with smart shops, you'll find **Musée Cantini** (at 19 rue Grignan, open daily Wednesday to Monday) housed in a late 17th-century mansion. This collection is dedicated to 20th-century art and various artists' views of Marseille. On entering you are greeted by a fine **Signac** (*L'Entrée du port de Marseille*) and a sombre view of the port by **Derain**. Among the collection's fine works are several paintings by **Dufy**, **Francis Bacon**, **Le Corbusier** and **Dubuffet**.

Quartier Longchamp *

The **Palais Longchamp** is the city's most prestigious building from the Second Empire and was built specifically to house both the Fine Arts Museum and the Natural History Museum.

The collection in the **Musée des Beaux-Arts** (Palais Longchamp, open daily Wednesday to Monday) is suitably impressive with Renaissance and later paintings from **Italy** (the first one you see is a lovely and large Perugino of the *Holy Family with Saint Anne*), Dutch work (look at Rubens' rather contrived *Hunting for Boar*) and, of course, an excellent collection of **French** work from the 17th–19th centuries. One room is devoted to the works of Marseille's talented sculptor, painter and architect, Pierre Puget. There is also a large section reserved for **drawings** (entry by appointment only).

CHÂTEAU D'IF

Just beyond the limits of the harbour, a small group of barren white islands rise from the sea. These are accessible by regular boat service from Le Vieux Port. The most visited are the Archipelago du Frioul and the Château d'If, built as a fortress under François I in 1524 and later used as an island prison for political prisoners (including the notorious Count Mirabeau). Thanks to Alexandre Dumas' *Count of Monte Cristo* the island became known internationally.

Below: *The Musée Cantini displays a good collection of modern art within its elegant 17th-century walls.*

Below: *The limpid waters
of the Calanques are very
popular with visitors.*

Les Calanques ★★★

Between Marseille and Cassis lie the picturesque
calanques. These are a series of bays and fjord-like inlets
slicing into the white limestone cliffs and ending, in some
instances, in small isolated beaches. Visually they are
stunning. The light coloured sea-bed creates translucent
turquoise waters while their steep sides, in many places
impossible to scale, are punctuated by the occasional
Aleppo pine. Boat trips from Cassis and (in summer)
Marseille, take visitors around their shores. Access routes
that crisscross the hilltops near the calanques are closed
in summer to reduce the fire risk.

Cassis ★★

Known for its chalky limestone and its wine, Cassis is a
gem of a village hidden between the steep hills of a
calanque. Its stone has been quarried for centuries and
one can still see the remains of structures that were used
to slide the blocks onto sailing ships bound for distant
shores. The white wine produced in Cassis is very good
and said to complement the local seafood. To the east of
Cassis, beyond its two sandy beaches, lies the western-
most tip of the red-coloured Massif de la Sainte-Baume
which, at 416m (1340ft), has the highest cliffs in Europe.

Martigues ★

This small harbour town on
the southwestern fringe of a
saline marsh area, **Étang de
Berre**, has a seaside atmosphere. Its medieval town
centre, picturesque market
stalls and a small marina,
tucked securely away on the
north shore of the Canale
de Caronte, are all typically
Provençal – in direct contrast
to the ugly refineries and
industrial area in the southern area of the étang.

AIX-EN-PROVENCE

One of France's most popular provincial towns, Aix is a place with undeniable atmosphere. It was founded by the Romans in 122BC who named it Aquae Sextiae for its spa.

Aix, as it is commonly known, boasts not one single outstanding monument – though it has a number of interesting sights – yet its mellow, ancient streets, unexpected fountains, ochre-coloured buildings and festive atmosphere never fail to charm. It is a youthful town thanks to its large transient student population, and an elegant one, known for superb cultural events such as the July *Festival d'Aix*. Part of Aix's attraction lies in settling at a café table in the shade of the plane trees and watching the ever-changing pageant of passers-by.

La Vieille Ville ★★★

A large avenue lined with massive shady plane trees, the 17th-century **cours Mirabeau** is Aix's axis, its point of reference. At its western end you'll come to the huge and refreshing **Fontaine de la Rotonde**, home to the town's tourist office. On the south side, stately mansions (some turned into administrative buildings) and smart shops contrast with the bustling cafés and restaurants that claim the pavement on the sunny north side of the Cours. Look out for *Le Café de deux garçons*, a Cézanne meeting place.

Above: *The fountain, La Rotonde, is a city landmark in Aix-en-Provence.*

THE SPECTACULAR DRIVE

The route between **La Ciotat** and **Cassis**, via the mountainside, is one of the most impressive drives in southern Provence. The road climbs from the naval town of La Ciotat through a series of hairpin bends, up to the top of the cliffs from where the views of the coast and calanques are spectacular on a clear day.

As you wend your way through the romantic, narrow and often pedestrian-only paved streets north of the Cours, you'll find the **Hôtel de Ville** (visit it on flower market mornings: Tuesday, Wednesday or Saturday) with its 17th-century Italianate façade. The place is largely taken up with cafés – as is much of old Aix – when the market is not operative.

Beyond the Hôtel de Ville, along rue Gaston de Saporta and on the **place de l'Université**, lies the **Cathédrale Saint-Sauveur** built on the foundations of the original Roman town. This ancient (and, from the exterior, odd-looking) building is a treasure trove. On entering the cathedral, note the highly ornate Gothic portal and the three naves: one each in the Roman, Gothic and Baroque styles. Spend time in the magnificent 12th-century **cloisters**, or the octagonal 5th-century **baptistry** built with Roman columns, and have a look at the famous *Burning Bush* by Nicolas Froment.

Opposite: *Open to visitors – Cézanne's studio in Aix is much as he left it.*

The **Musée des Tapisseries** (at place des Martyrs de la Résistance, open morning and afternoon, Wednesday to Monday) in the old archbishop's palace exhibits an impressive collection of French 17th- and 18th-century tapestries, including one depicting the adventures of Don Quixote that was woven in 1735.

Quartier Mazarin ✶✶

Created at the end of the 1640s by Archbishop **Michel Mazarin**, brother of the more famous Cardinal Mazarin, this *quartier* of coffee- and honey-coloured buildings is in direct contrast to La Vieille Ville. The streets are laid out to a grid plan and the blocks hide gardens in their centres with tumbling vines and creepers that can only just be glimpsed. Amid this lies the modern College Mignet, built on the foundations of the College Bourbon, where Cézanne and his friend Émile Zola studied, and the beautifully renovated Saint-Jean de Malte (slip in and have a look at the stained-glass windows and Delacroix's small painting of *Christ on the Cross*).

Adjoining Saint-Jean de Malte, the **Musée Granet** (located on rue Cardinale, open daily in summer) is where, apart from the interesting archaeological finds from Entremont, there are eight paintings and three watercolours by **Cézanne** and works by other notable French painters such as Granat, Géricault, Le Nain and Philippe de Champaigne, as well as various Flemish and Italian masters.

Atelier Cézanne **

A 15-minute walk out of the centre of town and up the hillside brings you to the **Atelier Cézanne**, situated in the house where the artist lived at the beginning of the 20th century. From this comfortable home with its lovely tree-filled garden and distant views of Mont Sainte-Victoire, Cézanne painted a number of canvases, including various views of the spectacular mountain.

ÉMILE ZOLA (1840–1902)

Although he was born in Paris, Émile Zola's family moved to Aix-en-Provence when he was just three. Four years later the death of his father dealt the child a major blow, but his friendship with classmate, Paul Cézanne, provided some solace. He failed his *baccalaureat* twice and gave up his studies, becoming an art critic for *l'Evénement Illustré* in 1866. With the publication of *Rougon-Macquart*, a series of 20 novels, Zola became a celebrity. His waning friendship with Cézanne ended with the publication of his novel, *l'Oeuvre*, the thinly fictitious story of a failed artist. In 1898 Zola wrote his famous article, *J'accuse*, during the infamous Dreyfus Affair, one of France's greatest scandals. Just four years later he died in Paris.

Below: *The craggy flanks of Mont Sainte-Victoire.*

PAUL CÉZANNE (1839–1906)

One of the greatest painters of the 19th century, Paul Cézanne was born in Aix-en-Provence. Abandoning his university studies, he went to Paris in 1861 and devoted himself to painting. He befriended Camille Pisarro and was initially much influenced by him, but by the 1870s he had turned towards Impressionism. Cézanne exhibited his work at various of the great Impressionist exhibitions but began exploring the use of colour in a different, more subtle way, using it as his key to modelling the subjects. He returned to Provence on the death of his father in 1886. By 1900, he was an acknowledged master, much revered by the younger generation. During his last years he worked out of Aix, frequently painting but rarely finishing the panoramic views of Mont Sainte-Victoire which he could see from his home and studio.

BEYOND AIX-EN-PROVENCE

Aix is a central point from which a number of interesting sites can be explored. You can follow Cézanne's footsteps into the magnificent wooded area around Mont Sainte-Victoire, make the short trip to Salon-de-Provence and Abbaye de Silvacane, or take a fast bus and visit Marseille and the coast.

Mont Sainte-Victoire ★★

Minutes east of the Quartier Mazarin, a different atmosphere unfurls. Here are fragrant pine forests, a narrow winding road and undulating hills. Glimpsed through the pines rises the familiar form, sometimes grey, sometimes white, of Mont Sainte-Victoire. This is Cézanne territory and, although the woods have changed and many new buildings have risen, the beauty of the barren mountain and the pine forests endures. As you approach the mountain the soil changes colour and becomes a deep almost blood-red, matching the colourful parachutes of some of those hang-gliders who hurl themselves off the summit of Mont Sainte-Victoire. The road continues up to the plateau around Saint-Antonin-sur-Bayon, where you can stop for a light meal. You can return to Aix via Châteauneuf-le-Rouge.

Salon-de-Provence *

Better known for its airforce academy and crack flying team, **La Patrouille de France**, Salon-de-Provence has, nevertheless, an ancient heart and some fine buildings. The centre of Salon is dominated by the oldest feudal castle in Provence. **Château de l'Empéri** (open Wednesday to Monday) houses a magnificent collection of over 10,000 items of armoury and arms, displayed with the help of 150 lifelike models, including 18 horses. The Napoleonic years are particularly well-documented. Nearby, the 13th-century church of **Saint-Michel** is a little gem, its ancient portal a fine piece of medieval stone masonry. To the north of town, passing along rue du Maréchal Joffre, lies the **Collégiale Saint-Laurent**, an imposing 14th-century building about which Louis XIV is said to have exclaimed: *This is my kingdom's most beautiful chapel!* On your way back to the main street, **cours Victor Hugo**, note the attractive **Fontaine Adam de Craponne**, dedicated to the Renaissance civil engineer of the same name.

It was in Salon that Nostradamus lived his last years. His house is now a museum. **Maison de Nostradamus** (on rue Nostradamus, open Sunday afternoon to Friday) is open to visitors. Enlivened with wax statues of the famous astrologer/doctor, it documents the remarkable life of this gifted scholar.

Abbaye de Silvacane *

One of three Cistercian abbeys constructed in the south of France, this is perhaps the most stark – its already austere interior is mostly empty. Built as a monastery in the 12th century, just outside today's Salon-de-Provence, it was abandoned by the 15th century though the chapel area continued to serve as a church for the local community. The cloister is its most attractive aspect: double columns holding the arches and a well for ablutions. The refectory was added in the 14th century. Interestingly, although the monks slept close together, the upper-level dormitory is so vast that it could have accommodated five times as many brothers.

Above: *A gigantic wall painting of Nostradamus in Salon-de-Provence.*

NOSTRADAMUS (1503–66)

Born Michel de Nostre Dame, this celebrated astrologer and son of Saint-Rémy-de-Provence lived for many of his later years in Salon-de-Provence. He received a doctorate in medicine from Montpellier University in 1533, and in 1546 discovered a remedy against the plague. He was given the name Nostradamus in 1550 and in 1555 published the first of his *Les Centuries*, a series of theses and predictions that made him famous but was banned by the Vatican. He died in 1566 and is commemorated with a simple stone inscription in the church of **Saint-Laurent** in Salon-de-Provence.

ARLES

Arles was the Rome of the north. Capital of the Gallo-Roman empire – Spain, Britain and France – it offered its citizens all the comforts of Rome and a climate not too radically different. More recently, Provençal poet Frédéric Mistral and Dutch painter Vincent Van Gogh have rendered the town famous. Its position as one of the major and most interesting historical sites in Provence is assured.

Roman Arles ***

There is still much of Roman Arles to see. The largest monument is the oval-shaped **Arènes**, an amphitheatre extending 136x107m (just over 150x125 yards) and capable of housing some 20,000 spectators when it was built in AD90. Despite its slightly ruined state it still thrives as a place of entertainment, these days for musical concerts and the town's traditional bullfights – its *Cocarde d'Or*, a Provençal game of speed and bravery with Camargue-raised bulls. These are held at Easter, during the first week of July, and for the Féria du Riz in September. Nearby you'll see the **Théâtre Antique**, a hemispherical Roman building used for theatre. This, too, is still used for performances such as the impressive annual **Féria d'Été** in July, when the Arlesiennes and their Provençal sisters don beautiful traditional costumes and parade through the streets to the theatre.

A fine Romanesque church in the central place de la Republique, the **Église** and its **Cloître Saint-Trophime** boast some extraordinarily well-executed and well-preserved sculpture, starting at the magnificent portal with apostles and finishing in the tranquil cloister where the capitals and statues are particularly noteworthy.

Wandering through the narrow town streets and across the shady places you'll come to the **Museon Arlaten** (Hôtel Laval-Castellane, rue de la République, open daily) created by Frédéric Mistral with the help of his Nobel prize-monry to safeguard and uphold the interest of all things Provençal. Among the dimly lit exhibits are some beautiful paintings and drawings.

The **Musée de l'Arles Antique** (av de la Première, Division Française Libre, open daily in summer, closed Tuesday in winter) houses antiquities in an ultra-modern building. This is the place to see the legacy of old Arles, an Arles that was inhabited from prehistory to the end of the Roman Empire. It is very well presented and a pleasure to explore. Another historic site (a 10-minute walk from town) is the fascinating **Les Alyscamps** necropolis, where the dead were buried from Roman times to the Middle Ages. Back in town take a look at the 4th-century AD **Thermes de Constantin**, the remains of Constantine's baths.

Although there is not one painting by Vincent Van Gogh in the south of France, his presence is fêted. The **Fondation Vincent Van Gogh–Arles** has a fine collection of reproductions, while **L'Espace Van Gogh** (located in the old Hôtel-Dieu where he was cared for after cutting off his ear) also sells cards, posters and various books about the master. **Café Van Gogh** (place du Forum) was the subject for his famous dusk painting of a café with a yellow canopy.

ABBAYE DE MONTMAJOUR

This high-profile abbey is visible for miles around, rising on a rocky outcrop above rice, sunflowers and Camargue horses. Starting as a simple chapel around the crypt and finishing, in 1791, with just a handful of Benedictine monks, 800 years of monastic life passed between its walls. Of particular interest in this solid, honey-coloured abbey is the simplicity of design, the beautiful **capitals** and **gargoyles** supporting the vaulted cloisters, and the oddly belligerent fortified tower dating from 1369 – a time when brigands devastated much of the countryside.

Opposite: *The bloodless cocarde bullfighting in the arena at Arles is a spectacle of bravery and agility where the bull is often the winner.*

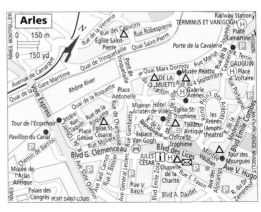

LES ALPILLES

The chalky-white limestone Alpilles, a chain of hills some 24km (nearly 15 miles) long from east to west, rise above a fertile olive and vine growing area. Within their folds some beautiful homes and interesting old towns lie hidden. The spectacular small range of hills changes colour and aspect under different weather conditions.

Saint-Rémy-de-Provence **

It was the Greeks who first settled here, but the classical legacy visible today is definitely Roman. On the road to Les-Baux, the remains of the Græco-Roman town of **Glanum** (today's Rémy) reveal a sophisticated settlement that thrived until AD260. It is one of the major classical sites in the south of France. The fabulously intact **mausoleum** and **triumphal arch** are just outside the necropolis, while the town of Glanum itself (which lay below an olive grove until some 60 years ago) is a fascinating mixture of ruined Roman residences, civic buildings and temples.

The town of Rémy (birthplace of Nostradamus) is a circular settlement of narrow stone streets lined with Provençal shops and cafés. Look out for the **Centre d'Art Présence Van Gogh**, an exhibition space with a rotating exhibition dedicated to the artist who spent time in the psychiatric hospital just outside town. Also visit the **Hôtel de Sade** (the same family as the infamous Marquis), built on the ruins of some Roman baths but now housing archaeological exhibits from Glanum.

Below: This impressive triumphal arch near Glanum was constructed by the Romans.

Les-Baux-de-Provence **

The village dates back to its medieval castle, which was built on a jagged outcrop (the word *baux* means escarpments), where it presided over the wide Rhône plains and afforded extensive vistas towards the sea. The 7ha (nearly 17-acre) **château** (open daily) still offers spectacular views and exhibits a number of medieval items of warfare including a catapult and ram which saw service here. Amid the white limestone blocks around which the castle's few buildings were constructed, are the remains of **troglodyte homes** – complete with panoramic views, stone cupboards and shelves.

Above: *Nestling in the folds of the craggy outcrops known as Les-Baux, is the pretty town of Les-Baux-de-Provence.*

The village of Les-Baux has been carefully restored to become one of France's prettiest. Hardly an electrical wire in sight, well-pointed stones, plenty of Provençal shops and some excellent restaurants.

The fatigue of climbing the sometimes steep and narrow streets is compensated by the fine views from the castle. For a panoramic sight, take the road marked 'Massane' up to the *table d'orientation*.

Beaucaire *

As you climb through the fir trees towards Beaucaire castle on a fine day, you may well catch sight of a falcon or an owl spreading its wings above the towers. This ruined castle is now the venue for an impressive flying display of birds of prey. Look out over the River Rhône towards Tarascon, and you will see yet another sturdy castle on the opposite bank.

Tarascon *

Separated from Beaucaire by the Rhône (now unlike in Roman days linked by modern bridges), this medieval town is known for its Souleïado factory, and its solid square Renaissance **castle** surrounded by a grass-filled moat. This was built for the dukes of Anjou and was often frequented by 'Good' King René.

Above: *The romance of the Camargue is upheld by its herds of white horses.*

LA CAMARGUE

This vast area of wetland, where the myriad fingers of the River Rhône delta fragment into the Mediterranean Sea, is one of the country's richest natural resources, and part of it has been preserved by the creation of a nature reserve where man and beast live together. The Camargue has an air of romance for most people – wild, white horses, vast herds of cattle, gypsies' caravans, pink flamingos and desolate beaches.

Parc Naturel Régional de Camargue ★★

The Camargue is an area where the bull is king and time-honoured traditions endure. Man has made use of the environment for herding his *manades* (livestock), planting rice in its basins, drying the saline waters in pans to harvest salt, and growing fruit and vegetables in the fertile Rhône estuary. The 85,000ha (200,000-acre) **Parc Naturel Régional de Camargue** comprises parts of the Camargue plain and parts of the Petite Camargue around Aigues-Mortes (the town is not actually part of Provence, but this area is just as fascinating and sometimes easier to access).

Flora and Fauna

Beyond the fields of sunflowers, groves of peach trees and viridian rice fields, the Camargue stretches without the slightest relief until the delta and its canals reach the sea. In parts nourished by fresh water, there are low trees, rushes, salt-loving plants, many flowers (in spring

AIGUES-MORTES

Some 34km (50 miles) from Saintes-Maries, across the Petit Rhône and Petite Camargue, and rising above the pink salt pans lies this perfectly walled medieval town, complete with un-broken ramparts, towers and gates. It was built around 1300 by **King Louis IX**, (later made a saint) as he wanted a port on the Mediterranean. Since those days the land has risen and the town is no longer on the shoreline. Although rather touristy, it still manages to retain its charm. Aigues-Mortes is also the headquarters of the Baleine Company, France's largest producer of sea salt. Visits to the salt works are a popular excursion.

there are, for instance, abundant yellow irises, tamarisk, narcissus, asphodels and thistles) and scrub; in other areas the water and alluvial deposits triumph (the Rhône discharges over 20 million cubic metres per annum), and shallow pans filled with mud and saline deposits stretch to the horizon.

These wetland areas are superb for birders. Apart from the 30,000 pairs of flamingos which breed annually on the **Étang du Fangassier** and forage during the day all throughout the Camargue, there are avocets, greater flamingos, kingfishers, marsh harriers, hoopoes, bee eaters, herons, slender-billed gulls, storks, countless waders and stints.

By far the most visible fauna of the Camargue is its tough **white horses**. Grey-brown when young, they turn white at approximately 7 years of age. Then there are the famous black bulls of the Camargue, fierce and dangerous, herded by the *gardians* (cowboys). On a smaller scale, there are rabbits, beavers and coypu, as well as small rodents.

Saintes-Maries-de-la-Mer *

This small town holds a special place in the hearts of the devout gypsy population. The belief is that Mary Magdalene, Mary Jacobea (the Virgin's sister) and Mary Salome left the Holy Land in AD39 and disembarked here with, among others, their black servant Sarah. In the castellated medieval church of the Three Saints Mary, a veritable fortress from the exterior and a tranquil simple retreat within, is the statue of Saint Sarah, the patron saint of gypsies. Each May the town overflows with gypsy families and caravans from France and beyond, as the celebrated statue is paraded through the streets.

EXPLORING THE CAMARGUE OFF-PISTE

One of the most interesting ways to discover the Camargue is by taking a small tour in a four-wheel-drive vehicle along tracks that are normally closed to the public. **Le Gitan** runs daily trips led by knowledgeable local Camarguais from Saintes-Maries-de-la-Mer. For further information, tel: 04 90 97 89 33.

Below: *The impenetrable exterior of Notre-Dame-de-la-Mer, at Saintes-Maries-de-la-Mer.*

PONT DU GARD

This magnificent Roman aqueduct straddles the **River Gardon** and was built under the rule of Roman Emperor Claudius in the middle of the 1st century to provide the increasingly large town of Nîmes with a constant supply of water. It forms part of a 50km-long (some 30 miles) water-bearing canal which leads to Nîmes from the Eure spring in Uzès via many obstacles. It took 10–15 years to complete and is made of a chalky limestone. Today, the aqueduct forms part of a fine wooded park punctuated by large lumps of stone and beaches beside the river. It is an ideal place to celebrate a summer picnic.

NÎMES

Its classical past has taught Nîmes about fine architecture. At the crossroads of the Cevennes and the Camargue, of Languedoc and Provence, this elegant city has melded Mediterranean and provincial styles to produce a city of fine architecture, much of it made of pale honey-coloured limestone, complete with classical details such as architraves and pediments. The small, cobbled streets and pocket-sized squares of the **Vieille Ville**, around the **cathedral** or the **place de l'Horloge**, mark the part of Nîmes dating from the 17th and 18th centuries. On its edges, classical and contemporary Nîmes rub shoulders comfortably.

Maison Carrée ★★★

One of the most complete legacies of the Roman world, this beautiful temple (situated at place Carrée, open daily) was dedicated to Caius and Lucius Cæsar (respectively the grandson and adopted son of Augustus), both of whom died young. It is believed to date from about AD5 and was based on the Temple of Apollo in Rome. Beautiful columns, Corinthian capitals and a (reconstructed) roof give this rather small building immense presence. It has been known, erroneously, as the Maison Carrée (or square house) since the 16th century.

Opposite this temple is a modern 'temple' to the past. Built by distinguished British architect Norman Foster, the **Carrée d'Art** (place Carrée, closed Tuesday), this state-of-the-art glass-and-steel building is a fitting stage for the city's fine **contemporary art museum**.

Nîmes

Les Arènes ★★★

The best-preserved amphitheatre in the Roman world, this 60m-high (200ft), two-storey arena capable of seating 20,000 has traded its gladiators and wild beasts for toreadors and bulls. Now one of France's premier bullrings, it was built in the 1st century AD and it is still used today, both for bullfighting and to host concerts.

Other **Roman remains** include the ramparts, some 5km (just over 3 miles) in length and rising to a mighty 9m (30ft) in height. Today's **Porte d'Auguste** was where the Via Domitia entered Nîmes from the Roman town of Beaucaire (*see* page 45). At the other end of town is the Roman **Porte de France**, previously known as the Porte de Espagne, as it opened out onto the Via Domitia leading to Spain.

Above: *Proud Roman architecture: the Maison Carrée in Nîmes.*

Museums ★

Housed in a 17th-century building (located at 18bis bd Amiral Courbet, open Tuesday to Sunday), the **Musée Archéologique** amassed exhibits from the Iron Age, as well as Roman and medieval times, and has a large selection of Roman funerary glassware. The **Musée du Vieux Nîmes** (place aux Herbes, opening times as above) puts the spotlight on life in Nîmes since the end of the Middle Ages – an interesting and unusual slant.

Jardins de la Fontaine ★

This is a pleasant garden consisting of canals and shady trees, with a large fountain marking one corner. In its centre is the **Temple of Diana**, a small building which might have served as a library, or possibly as cult room in the imperial sanctuary.

Excursions

Nîmes is a good base if you wish to explore the region. Just to the northeast is the splendid **Pont du Gard**, while the Gorges de Ardèche, Villeneuve-lès-Avignon and Fort Saint-André are all within easy reach.

PARC ORNITHOLOGIQUE DE PONT GAU

A 60ha (150-acre) wetland park just outside **Saintes-Maries**, this ornithological reserve is an ideal way to get to know the birds of the Camargue. The three trails are well-marked, with explanatory boards giving excellent background information on the birds and plants. You can hope to see some of the 170 species of birds, including (seasonally) ducks, herons, egrets, ibis, storks, geese, avocets, stints, bee eaters, and, of course, pink flamingos. Caged birds (often recuperating after injury) include storks, owls, eagles and other raptors. There is also a herd of cattle which can be observed from a hide at the edge of the park. The park is open year-round, except Christmas day. From the end of August to May the numbers of birds are at their highest. For further information tel: 04 90 97 82 62.

Bouches-du-Rhône at a Glance

Best Times To Visit

July sees the International Festival of Dance in Aix-en-Provence. Marseille's **Foire Internationale** is in September as is the **Fête des Vins** in Cassis, while the **Fiesta des Suds** is held in October. Autumn and spring are fine times to visit. Winter is great for birding in the Camargue.

Getting There

Marseille has a good **international airport** with flights from Britain, Paris and other French airports. Buses runs every 20 minutes from the airport to **Gare Saint-Charles** in the centre of town. The city is connected by the toll-paying A7 motorway to Lyon (314km/196 miles) and Paris (772km/480 miles), and by the E80 and A8 to Nice (191km/120 miles). The *département* has good *routes nationales* and well-maintained *routes départementales* though these are congested in summer. **Bus services** link Marseille with Paris, Nice and Barcelona. For details, tel: 04 91 08 16 40. **Nîmes** is directly linked with London, Stansted, by daily Ryanair flights. For information call the Aéroport de Nîmes-Arles-Camargue on tel: 04 66 70 06 88 or look up their website: www.ryanair.com Marseille is on one of France's main **railway lines**. The high-speed TGV (*Train à Grande Vitesse*) and other intercity trains (*Grandes Lignes*) lead to Paris (around 3 hours), or westwards

to Montpellier and Spain, and eastwards to Nice and Italy. For railway information tel: 08 36 35 35 35; or 08 36 35 35 39 for English-language operators.

Getting Around

Marseille's *métro* operates from 05:00–21:00 daily. **Buses** serve most parts of the city. A *ticket touristic* gets you to the sights. Other towns and villages in the Bouches-du-Rhône are small enough to explore on foot. **Taxis** are available, but not cheap. For travel between towns and villages there are local **bus services**, though the frequency may not be more than once daily. Check at the tourist offices in each town for schedules. It is easiest to hire a car and go exploring yourself.

Where to Stay

Luxury

Hôtel Sofitel Marseille Vieux-Port, 36 bd Charles Livon, Marseille, tel: 04 91 15 59 00, fax: 91 15 59 50, e-mail: HO542@accor-hotels.com Harbour views, restaurant.
Hostellerie du Vallon de Valrugues, chemin de Canto Cigalo, St-Rémy-de-Provence, tel: 04 90 92 04 40, fax: 90 92 44 01, e-mail: vallon.valruges@wanadoo.fr Old mansion, good restaurant.
Villa Galici, av de la Violette, Aix-en-Provence, tel: 04 42 23 29 23, fax: 42 96 30 45, e-mail: gallici@relaischateaux.fr In a former villa, fine restaurant. North of the *centre historique*.

Abbaye de Sainte-Croix, route de Val de Cuech, Salon-de-Provence, tel: 04 90 56 24 55, fax: 90 56 31 12, e-mail: saintecroix@relaischateaux.fr A 12th-century abbey. Superb location, 5 minutes from Salon.
Hôtel Imperator Concorde, Quai de la Fontaine, Nîmes, tel: 04 66 21 90 30, fax: 66 67 70 25, e-mail: hotel.imperator@wanadoo.fr A smart, mid-sized hotel near the historic centre of Nîmes.
Hôtel Jules César, bd des Lices, Arles, tel: 04 90 52 52 52, fax: 90 52 52 53, e-mail: julescesar@calva.net Former convent, now luxury hotel and excellent restaurant.

Mid-range

Mercure Beauvau Vieux-Port, 4 rue Beauvau, Marseille, tel: 04 91 54 91 00, fax: 91 54 15 76, e-mail: HI293@accor-hotels.com Historic building with harbour views, right in the centre.
La Maison, Domaine de Bournissac, Monté de'Eyragues, Paluds-de-Noves, tel: 04 90 90 25 25, fax: 90 90 25 26, e-mail: annie@ lamaison-a-bournissac.com Delightful *mas* (farmhouse), now small hotel. Restaurant.
Auberge Cavalière, route d'Arles, Saintes-Maries-de-la-Mer, tel: 04 90 97 88 88, fax: 04 90 97 84 07. A traditional whitewash-and-thatch hotel; also has Camargue-style bungalows, butting onto lakes and marshes.

Bouches-du-Rhône at a Glance

BUDGET

Hôtel Azur, 24 cours Franklin Roosevelt, Marseille, tel: 04 91 42 74 38, fax: 04 91 47 27 91. Small, friendly family-run hotel.

Hôtel Mascotte, av de la Cible, Aix-en-Provence, tel: 04 42 37 58 58, fax: 42 37 58 59. Modern, pool and free parking.

Hostellerie de la Crémaillère, rue Tony Garnier, Carnoux, tel: 04 42 73 71 52, fax: 42 73 67 26. Small hotel north of Cassis.

Hôtel des Quatre Dauphins, 54 rue Roux Alphéran, Aix-en-Provence, tel: 04 42 38 16 39, fax: 42 38 60 19. In Quartier Mazarin, small, charming hotel.

Hôtel Le Prieuré, route des Alpes, Aix-en-Provence, tel: 04 42 21 05 23, fax: 42 21 60 56. A converted 17th-century priory overlooking a lovely garden.

Hostellerie Le Chalet Fleuri, 15 rue F. Mistral, St-Rémy-de-Provence, tel: 04 90 92 03 62, fax: 90 92 60 28. Just minutes from the old heart of town.

Hôtel de la Muette, 15 rue des Suisses, Arles, tel: 04 90 96 15 39, fax: 90 49 73 16. Small, central and full of character.

WHERE TO EAT

LUXURY

L'Ambassade des Vignobles, 49 place aux Huiles, Marseille, tel: 04 91 33 00 25. Renowned selection of wines marrying perfectly with Provençal cuisine.

Abbaye de Sainte-Croix (see Where to Stay). Fine restaurant.

Lou Marques, Hôtel Jules César (see Where to Stay). Outstanding, innovative cuisine.

MID-RANGE

Chez Caruso, 158 quai du Port, Marseille, tel: 04 91 90 94 04. Alongside Vieux-Port, renowned for its fish and bouillabaisse.

Chez Vincent, 25 rue Glandevès, Marseille, tel: 04 91 33 96 78. Italy meets Marseille with fresh produce.

Au Basilic Gourmand, 6 rue Griffon, Aix-en-Provence, tel: 04 42 96 08 58. Pleasant ambience and excellent cuisine.

Chez Maxime, 12 place Ramus, Aix-en-Provence, tel: 04 42 26 28 51. Indoor-outdoor dining, fine wines.

Brasserie Nord Pinus, 6 rue du Palais, Arles, tel: 04 90 93 02 32. Traditional brasserie.

BUDGET

La Panier des Arts, 3 rue du Petit Puits, Marseille, tel: 04 91 56 02 32. Typically Marseillaise.

La Pizza, 3 rue Aude, Aix-en-Provence, tel: 04 42 26 22 17. Street-side pizzas in colourful corner, just a minute from cours Mirabeau. Good value.

Laurane et Sa Maison, 16 rue Victor Leydet, Aix-en-Provence, tel: 04 42 93 02 03. Delightful rustic atmosphere for good, southern French cuisine.

L'Olivade, 12 rue du Château, St-Rémy-de-Provence, tel: 04 90 92 52 74. Provençal cuisine.

Lou Calèu, 22 rue Porte de Laure, Arles, tel: 04 90 49 71 77. Typical Provençal dishes.

SHOPPING

Good buys include Provençal fabrics, table linen, food (olives and olive oils, skeins of garlic and onions, cheeses) and Marseille's famous soap, *savon de Marseille*.

USEFUL CONTACTS

Office de tourisme, 4 La Canebière, Marseille, tel: 04 91 13 89 00.

Office de tourisme, place Jean Jaurès, Saint-Rémy-de-Provence, tel: 04 90 92 05 22.

Office de tourisme, 6 rue Auguste, Nîmes, tel: 04 66 67 29 11.

Office de tourisme, bd des Lices, Arles, tel: 04 90 18 41 20.

Office de tourisme, Saintes-Maries-de-la-Mer, tel: 04 90 97 82 55.

Les Quatres Maries, boat trips on the sea and up the Petit Rhône to unspoiled areas of the Camargue, tel: 04 90 97 70 10, fax: 04 90 97 81 96.

MARSEILLE	J	F	M	A	M	J	J	A	S	O	N	D
AVERAGE TEMP. °F	44	46	50	55	62	70	75	74	69	60	51	46
AVERAGE TEMP. °C	6	7	10	12	16	21	23	23	20	15	10	7
HOURS OF SUN DAILY	4	6	6	8	9	10	11	10	8	6	5	4
RAINFALL in	1.6	1.6	1.6	1.6	1.6	0.8	0.4	0.8	2.4	3.5	2.8	1.9
RAINFALL mm	40	40	40	40	40	20	10	20	60	90	70	50
DAYS OF RAINFALL	1	1	1	1	2	3	1	2	2	3	1	1

3
Vaucluse

This *département* is the epitome of rural Provence. Numerous vineyards, lavender fields, rural market towns, medieval castles, Roman remains and a rugged mountain backdrop paint a colourful vista of Provence. The capital of the *département*, **Avignon**, is one of France's finest small towns. Its fortified walls rise high above the fast-running waters of the River Rhône, detaching the town from the wide plains around it. The popes of the early 14th century brought their court here and established a new papal seat, which was contested subsequently when Pope Gregory XI died in Rome. The antipopes stubbornly refused to relocate their court, and the Great Western Schism was fought out between Avignon and Rome.

The popes built themselves a castle (**Châteauneuf-du-Pape**) in their wine-growing area, which is now better known for its wine than for the building itself. Further to the north, the Romans left an impressive legacy in **Orange**, where to this day the theatre is still in use. **Vaison-la-Romaine** is another historic town with both Roman and medieval remains. **Carpentras** is known for its huge and fascinating market, and also as the town where the oldest synagogue in France is situated. The **Luberon**, well loved by many visitors, is the site of dozens of small *villages perchés*, tiny and often stunning settlements clinging precariously to the mountainside. Arguably the most spectacular of these is **Gordes**, but all of them afford sweeping panoramas of the region.

DON'T MISS

*** Le Palais des Papes: situated in Avignon.
*** Roman Theatre: witness Orange at festival time.
*** Gordes: medieval 'perched village'.
*** Ardeche: for its gorges.
** Vaison-la-Romaine: ancient Roman town.
** Châteauneuf-du-Pape: wine tasting.
* Carpentras market: a bustling weekly market.
* The Luberon: experience a hot-air balloon ride.

Opposite: *Gordes hugs the hillside and creates a striking profile as one of Provence's most photographed* villages perchés.

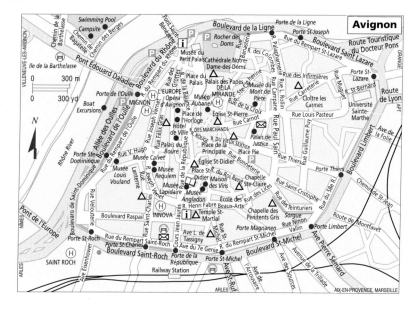

Avignon

Carpentras (see page 59)

Opposite: *Part of the medieval Papal Palace in Avignon.*

A LANDMARK MARKET

Carpentras (see page 59) is justly renowned for its fabulous and extensive **weekly market**, a Friday tradition that has been going so long it is now protected by law. In season (November to March), the market is known for its *diamants noirs* (truffles), but throughout the year it is a showcase of Provençal food and wines, honeys and fabrics, souvenirs and handicrafts. It takes place throughout the medieval heart of town, around Cathédrale Saint-Siffrein.

AVIGNON

The Vatican's most important city outside Rome, the walled city of Avignon was the papal seat from 1309–77. The popes brought new ideas, architects and an interest in the arts to this part of France, and much of the erudition and elegance still flourishes. Avignon is a sophisticated, beautifully laid-out city dominated by the papal palace, the **Palais des Papes**, and the **Cathédrale Notre-Dame-des-Doms** on one side of the huge traffic-free square. The city boasts several interesting museums, good shops (especially in the old quarter of town) and many restaurants and cafés.

Le Palais des Papes ***

Huge, almost fairytale-like in its medieval aspect, **le Palais des Papes** (place du Palais, open daily) towers over the city. Its austere walls of golden limestone are devoid of all but the most narrow arrow slits, and topped by battlements and towers. Built largely by popes **Benoît XII** (1334–42) and **Clement VI** (1342–52), it was home to nine popes and their predominantly male entourages, a seat of learning and religious jurisdiction throughout Christendom and a centre for arts in this, the *Altera Roma* (alternative Rome). Today, much of the interior is open daily to visitors, and audio guides bring alive the glory of the distant epoch.

Entering beneath the thin towers through the Port des Chapeaux, cross the courtyard and climb stairs to **La Salle Consistoire** (where portraits of Avignon's Popes stare at today's visitors) and the **Cour d'Honneur** (used for performances during the Avignon Festival). Take in the kitchens and hear the long shopping list for a papal banquet, walk through the popes' **private apartments** (with the delightful **fresco of hunting scenes** by Italian maestro, **Matteo Giovannetti**), and then leave by the **Grande Chapelle** where Giovannetti painted a number of beautiful ceiling frescoes.

Cathédrale Notre-Dame-des-Doms *

Next to the Palais, crowned by a dazzling gilt statue of the Virgin, the town's cathedral is a 12th-century monument where, among other notables, two popes are buried.

Musée du Petit Palais **

At the far end of the place du Palais lies this museum, once the residence of Avignon's archbishops. Open Wednesdays to Mondays, the 'little' medieval palace houses an excellent collection of medieval art, including 13th–16th-century **Italian paintings** and local Avignonaise **sculptural** works.

More Museums *

Musée Calvet (rue Joseph Vernet, open morning and afternoon, Wednesday to Monday) is housed in a beautiful 18th-century mansion and offers fine Renaissance paintings and a small collection of 19th- and 20th-century art, including **paintings** by **Claudel**, **Manet**,

---

LES CÔTES DU RHÔNE

One of France's best-known *appelation contrôlée*, the **Côtes du Rhône** comprise some very famous wines in a region that has been producing wine for 2000 years. The area encompasses 58,300ha (144,000 acres) and 163 communities through 6 *départements*, from Avignon in the south to Vienne in the north. Sixteen communities produce the superior wines (red, white or rosé) grouped under the *Côtes du Rhône Villages* appelation, among them wines from Saint-Gervais, Beaumes-de-Venise, Séguret and Saint-Pantaléon les Vignes. The most prestigious category is, however, the Cru, a label that only 13 villages are entitled to use. Among these are Châteauneuf-du-Pape (red and white wines), Gigongas (red and white), and on the western side of the Rhône Crozes Hermitage (red and white).

THEMED ROUTES

A number of routes are being promoted so that visitors can discover various aspects of Provençal culture. Among these are the **Route des Dentelles**, a round trip from Carpentras to Vaison-la-Romaine that passes either side of the Dentelles de Montmirail, the spiky, limestone outcrops; **Route des Vins** from Avignon to Vienne, or around Vacqueras, Gigondas and Séguret, to taste the wines of the Côtes du Rhône; the **Route de la Lavande** (Sénanque), following those beautiful fields of lavender; the **Route de l'Olivier** around Merindol-les-Oliviers and Buis-les-Baronnies wends though olive groves and past oil mills where the visitor can stop and see the oil production; the **Route de Sel** following the route that the mule salt trains took from Villefranche to Turin; and the **Route de l'Ochre**, north of the Luberon, starting in Apt, which takes in the extraordinary red cliffs of Roussillon and the Colorado de Rustrel ochre quarry.

Sisley and **Soutine**. **Musée Angladon** (5 rue Laboreur, open afternoon, Wednesday to Sunday) has a collection of 19th- and 20th-century works owned by the Fondation Angladon Dubrujeaud. Among the many treasures are paintings by **Picasso**, **Cézanne**, **Modigliani** and **Van Gogh**. The chapel of the **Musée Lapidaire**, formerly a 17th-century Jesuit college (27 rue de la République, same hours as Musée Calvet) houses **classical sculpture** and **antiquities**. If your interests lie in the decorative arts, don't miss the **porcelain** and **silverware** in the **Musée Louis Vouland**, 17 rue Victor Hugo (open the same hours as Musée Calvet).

Le Pont d'Avignon ★★

Correctly called Pont Saint-Bénézet, this broken bridge spans just half the River Rhône. Destroyed during the Crusade of the Albigeois in 1226, it is said to be the bridge in the famous song: *Sur le pont d'Avignon, on y danse …*

Châteauneuf-du-Pape ★★

The well-trodden route to the north from Avignon runs through the fertile Rhône valley and leads to Châteauneuf-du-Pape, a village better known today for its red wines than its papal **castle**. Built in 1317 by Pope John XXII, the castle is of moderate interest. The village, however, trades heavily on its *appellation contrôlée*, and scores of small wine producers open the doors to their caves, offering the visitor a chance to sample their rich and fairly expensive product.

Opposite: *Carved over 2000 years ago, this triumphal arch boasts some interesting sculpture.*
Right: *Celebrated in song, the ruins of the Pont Saint-Bénézet still stand on the Rhône.*

ORANGE

How lovely Orange must have looked when the Romans laid out their 70ha (173-acre) walled town on the banks of the River Meyne in 35BC. The House of Orange-Nassau, which governed not just the Netherlands but also, at one time, England and a small principality in France, sadly decided that the bricks of the ancient Roman outpost would serve well to reinforce its local domain. Hence, the vestiges of Roman Orange include only the **Théâtre Antique** (the site of the annual arts festival) and the **Arc de Triomphe**. Orange is at its best during the festival, but its colourful streets and cathedral invite exploration throughout the year.

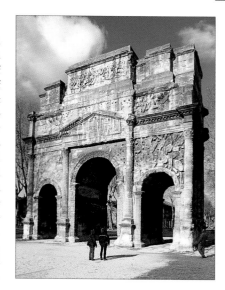

Théâtre Antique, the Roman Theatre ★★★

The Roman Theatre was built during 27–25BC under Emperor Augustus (whose statue presides over the arena), right up against a hill and with an impressive back wall. This hemispherical theatre (situated at place des Frères Mounet, open almost daily) is one of the Roman Empire's best preserved examples – only the top sections of the columns are lacking. The theatre was covered, as was customary in Roman theatres, by a moveable vellum awning that was anchored to the exterior by guy ropes. The theatre used to hold 10,000 people, though today it accommodates slightly less.

Arc de Triomphe ★★

Marooned in the middle of a busy road (the former Via Agrippa), the Roman Triumphal Arch with its three passageways, columns and architraves was dedicated to the **Gallic Legions** and then to **Emperor Tiberius**. Built around 20BC, it boasts some fine sculpture on its north face. Take time to look at the reliefs of marine items – anchors, galleons and tridents.

THE POPES' WINES

Within the ancient walls of the Palais des Papes, **La Bouteillerie du Palais des Papes** runs a small wine shop and tasting bar. The wines have been specially selected by the city's premier sommeliers to showcase the produce of Châteauneuf-du-Pape, the Côte du Rhone and other small *appelations* in Provence. This area has been making wine for nearly 700 years and the tradition is as old as the walls of the Palais itself. Knowledgeable staff are on hand to navigate your testing skills from light whites to the heavier aged reds from the popes' territory. All wines can be shipped. For more information, tel: 04 90 27 50 00, or website: http://www.palais-des-papes.com

BEYOND THE RHÔNE VALLEY

Traditionally considered a part of Provence (even though it is not, administratively speaking) the area west of the Rhône is just a short drive from Avignon or Orange.

Les Gorges de l'Ardeche ***

The region surrounding the River Ardeche is one of southern France's most visited natural attractions. The 120km (75-mile) river has, over the course of millennia, sliced through the white limestone hills on either side, cleaving a steep-sided course as it flows southeast to join the Rhône. The views from the top are magnificent – and much appreciated by hikers. In the upper reaches of the river, visitors can hire canoes and boats at **Vallon-Pont-d'Arc** and explore the river, passing under the much-photographed **Pont-d'Arc**, an arch in the form of a bridge. The river winds through the hills through an area designated as a national park, via the **Haute Corniche** (the river's most spectacular scenery with plenty of lookout points) to arrive some 6–9 hours later in Saint-Martin d'Ardeche.

Another region to explore is the nearby **Cèze** valley, which similarly offers canoeing at Saint-Ambroix.

Uzès **

Rising from the dried and sparse garrigue vegetation, lies the postcard-pretty village of Uzès. A small duchy harking back to the 15th century, its ancient walls have harboured, among others, writers Jean Racine (1639–99) and André Gide (1869–1951). The ducal building known as the **Duché** which occupies the centre of Uzès is a monument with some interesting ducal apartments, ancient towers and a fine Renaissance façade. The **cathedral** boasts an elaborate and elegant tower, the circular **Tour Fenestrelle**.

TO THE EAST OF THE RHÔNE

Various old settlements crown the hills in the Vaucluse, stretched apart by wide open expanses of countryside. Once wild, much is now tamed by agriculture and vineyards. The distant peak of Mont Ventoux, and the craggy outcrops that earned the sobriquet, Les Dentelles (lace), rise from this fertile landscape.

Carpentras *

At first encounter, there seems little remarkable about Carpentras, but it has a rich past and a superb weekly market. Although its roots go back to Roman times, and Pope Clément V and his cardinals passed much time here, the town is better known for its 14th-century **synagogue** (place Maurice Charretier, open Monday to Friday), the oldest in France and once the hub of the Jewish ghetto comprising over 1300 members. Small but dignified, it is an interesting place to visit.

Gothic **Cathédrale Saint-Siffrein** has the fascinating and heavily decorated **Porte Juive**, through which converted Jews passed for Mass. To the side of the cathedral and behind the 17th-century **Palais de Justice**, the **Arc de Triomphe** pays tribute to the town's Roman past.

Mont Ventoux **

The mistral often swirls through the land around Mont Ventoux, confirming its name 'windy mountain'. Chilling to the marrow, the wind is merciless, but has the advantage of clearing the sky and imbuing the landscape with a keen, brilliant light. Mont Ventoux rises to 1909m (6263ft) and is often snow-capped in winter. It is possible to reach the summit by car (snow permitting) where the views are out of this world. Keen **ramblers** can walk to the summit from either Malaucène, Bédoin or Brantes.

> **TAVEL**
>
> This small town is noted for its **vin rosé**, one of France's classic table wines. Visitors can taste this dry but full-bodied wine at the Cooperative de Tavel.

Opposite: *The natural arch, Pont du Arc, amid the Gorges de l'Ardeche.*
Below: *The southern and western slopes of Mont Ventoux produce some good wines.*

Below: *A section of the ruined Roman remains of Vasio Vocontiorum, today's Vaison.*

Les Dentelles de Montmirail ***

The lacy outcrops of white limestone breaking through the upper reaches of Montmirail are known as the Dentelles, from the word *dentelle* (meaning lace). This attractive terrain is a favourite for ramblers. A circular route of 50km (30 miles) takes the visitor through pretty hilltop villages, past sturdy castles clinging to rocky summits, across vineyards bearing the **Côte du Rhône** appellation, and past the lovely Roman town of Vaison, all the while affording excellent views.

The prettiest villages along this route include **Suzette**, **Séguret** (worth stopping for a pastis to appreciate its charms) and (slightly off the route) the beautifully restored little village of **Crillon-le-Brave**. Behind **Caromb**, the 12th-century château at **le Barroux** surveys the vineyards and olive groves spreading southward. The national road takes in **Gigondas** and **Vacqueyras**, both offering opportunities to sample local wines and the town of **Beaumes-de-Venise**, renowned for its muscat wines.

Vaison-la-Romaine **

Vaison was founded by the Celts of Voconces, but appropriated by the Romans in the 2nd century BC. The town prospered under the conquerors but fell into decline along with the Empire. Later inhabitants preferred higher land and moved across the River Ouvèze. Medieval Vaison is south of the river, gripping the sides of a rocky mountain, while Roman Vaison was laid out on the flatter northern side of the river. The two are joined by the **Pont Romain**.

The Roman remains (open daily) are extensive and lie on both sides of av Général de Gaulle. In the **Puymin Quarter** look out for the small **Roman theatre** hewn out of rock (used for Vaison's summer festival), the **House of Messii**, once home to a wealthy Roman family,

and **Pompey's Portico**, a
colonnaded building fre-
quented by the citizens. The
museum exhibits many items
found during excavation,
including marble statues of
Claudius, Hadrian and his
wife, Sabina.

The Villasse area of the
archaeological site reveals
the public baths and two
Roman villas, the **Maison au Dauphin** and the **Maison
au buste d'argent**, the latter named for the silver
sculpted portrait (3rd century AD) found here, now on
display in the museum.

Isle-sur-la-Sorgue *

With the babbling Sorgue river running a ring around
it, Isle-sur-la-Sorgue is an appealing town of avenues
shaded by lofty plane trees and cooled by the fast-
flowing river. It used to be known for its tannery, fabric
weaving, and its grain and oil mills – 6 mill wheels still
bear witness to this era. Its fame today lies in the frenzy
which develops here each weekend as the stalls and
shops comprising its **antiques market** open their doors
and bargain hunters descend on the town, scouring the
transient stock of silver, furniture, artifacts, bric-à-brac
and china for a valuable item.

Fontaine-de-Vaucluse ***

The Romans dubbed this area the *Vallis clausa* (closed
valley) which gave this *département* its name. Sheer limestone hills cup this part of Provence, and from its heart
surges the River Sorgue, a fierce underground torrent
that bursts onto the landscape as one of the world's most
powerful fountainheads. It starts by welling up into a
limpid turquoise blue **pool**, (a 20-minute walk from the
village) which, after the winter rains, overflows downhill
into the village of Fontaine-de-Vaucluse. The various
splinters of the River Sorgue are used for generating

Above: *Known for its
rich Gigondas reds and its
Beaume-de-Venise muscat
wines, there is ample
opportunity to taste the
local produce of the
Dentelles region.*

> **WINE TASTING IN
> THE DENTELLES**
>
> That chalky soil under the
> Dentelles is excellent for
> producing wines.
> Predominantly reds, though
> boasting also with a very fine
> muscat wine, the wines from
> this area travel far and wide.
> Gigondas, Vacqueyras, Côte
> du Rhone and Beaumes-de-
> Venise: you can sample a
> wide selection of these at
> the friendly **Cave des
> Vignerons**, Route de Vaison
> la Romaine, Vacqueyras
> (tel: 04 90 65 84 54, open
> 08:00–12:00 and
> 14:00–18:00 daily).

Above: *Ballooning over the Luberon in the early morning affords wonderful views of the region.*

BALLOONING OVER THE LUBERON

For those seeking height, a ballooning company runs morning flights from Joucas, (a few kilometres east of Gordes) weather permitting. The direction the flight takes is entirely ruled by the light winds and it can last anything from 30–70 minutes. The balloons travel at low levels, skimming treetops and hovering over the sunflower and lavender fields. They are tracked by the ground team who bring guests back for a fine breakfast at Joucas. Booking is essential. For more details, tel: 04 90 05 76 77, fax: 04 90 05 74 39.

---

power and for turning the famous 14th-century **Moulin à Papier Vallis Clausa**, an ancient paper mill. Cafés and restaurants crowd its banks, souvenir stores sell postcards of the pleasing little village, and the **Musée Petrarque** pays homage to the 14th-century Italian poet, Francesco Petrarch, who pined for his lovely Laura in this village for 16 long years.

THE LUBERON

The only substantial range of mountains between the Mediterranean and the Alps, the Luberon is an unspoiled area of photogenic stone villages clinging to the hillsides, craggy limestone outcrops and an untamed highland area, a haven for nature lovers. The climate on the southern side is dry and Mediterranean; on the northern side, more humid and temperate.

The Luberon mountains divide neatly into two areas, either side of **Lourmarin** (where Albert Camus lived): the lower **Petit Luberon** to the west with its string of beautiful perched villages, and the spectacular grandeur of the **Grand Luberon** in the east, rising to its highest point, Mourre Nègre at 1125m (3690ft). At the western extreme of the region, the market town of Cavaillon provides an entry point to the area.

Parc Naturel Régional du Luberon **

Comprising some 140,000ha (345,940 acres) and stretching through a few score communities, this park was gazetted in 1977 to protect the wealth of flora and fauna and help develop controlled tourism in the area. To this end a number of information centres have been set up to assist the visitor.

Part of the reason this natural park is so diverse is because of its unusual structure – a mixture of white chalky rock and the deposits of ochre give rise to a rich ecosystem comprising evergreens, **cedar** and **oak forests** as well as garrigues, while these in turn provide protection for rare orchids, owls, Bonelli's eagle, lizards and wild boar. The area is also known for its **bories** (*see* panel, this page), unusual stone buildings, some 3000 in total, that are a feature of this landscape.

Apt ★

In Roman days **Apt** was a prosperous town. Today it is known for its fruit growing, jam making, ochre extraction and for the production of essence of lavender (the lavender fields between Saignon and Bonnieux are spectacular). It is also a good spot from which to discover the Parc Naturel Régional du Luberon. The **Maison du Parc Naturel Régional du Luberon**, located in an elegant 17th-century mansion in the town, is the park's visitor information centre and has an interesting paleontological section. Also in town, the 12th-century **cathedral** dedicated to Saint Anne merits a short visit. Apt has a vibrant Saturday market, ideal for stocking up on Provençal goodies and an excellent place to get a feel for true Provençal life.

A fascinating option for visitors who have a car is the **Ochre Route** (*see* page 56), which leaves from Apt and leads to the endearing and quite different village of **Roussillon**. It is painted a wonderfully rich red hue in keeping with its nearby ochre quarry, the so-called Colorado of the Luberon.

STONE HOMES

Over 3000 small stone buildings remain in the Luberon area. Known as **bories**, these round or rectangular windowless structures are created out of slabs of local limestone (no cement or filling), each layer sloping outwards slightly, and gradually curving inward to form a vault-like roof. This required a certain expertise, and specialist masons were responsible for their construction. The bories are believed to date back to the Stone Age, when the Ligurians inhabited the area. A visit to the social museum, the **Village des Bories** (open daily, tel: 04 90 72 02 08, fax: 04 90 72 04 39), just outside Gordes, puts these interesting buildings in perspective. Twenty have been renovated and the museum shows how they were used.

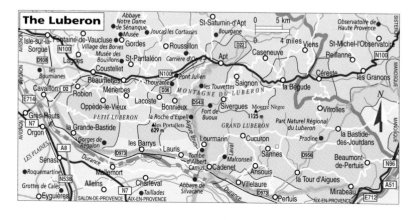

Bonnieux **

Perching high on a promontory, Bonnieux is another delightful and often photographed Provençal village. The villages of Lacoste and Gordes are visible just a few kilometres away. Crowning the village is the **Église Vieille**, the old church, which dates back to the 12th century, though most of it was added in the 15th, and from this high point the village fans out below.

Don't miss a visit to the **Musée de la Boulangerie**, a museum in a 17th-century building dedicated to the history of breadmaking with, among other items, some interesting old cartoons, moulds and prints. Just out of town is the **Forêt des Cèdres**, a sweet-smelling cedar forest with a mapped botanical track that makes a refreshing setting for a picnic.

Ménerbes **

This is a severe looking town and a stronghold of the Vaudois. Although it is not of any outstanding beauty, it has suffered less at the hands of tourism and has superb views over the plains towards Gordes.

Leaving the village, stop awhile on the plain and visit the **Musée du Tire-Bouchon**, (open daily in summer, morning and afternoon) for a look at the fascinating collection of corkscrews which reflect the tastes, needs and fancies of wine drinkers over the last 300 years.

Below: *Gordes is well situated for exploration of the Luberon region.*

Oppède-le-Vieux *

An unusual terraced village where the ancient stones hark back to medieval times (though the first traces of settlement actually date back to the Romans), Oppède was the property of the belligerent Baron de Oppède who is remembered for his war against the heretic Vaudois (in his zeal he annihilated nearly a dozen local villages). The fascination of Oppède is its ruined village, hidden *intramuros* behind the chic renovated limestone homes outside the walls.

Gordes ★★★

Rising steeply beyond the Calavon Valley, Gordes must be one of France's prettiest *villages perchés*. Echoing the limestone cliffs that mark the end of the Vaucluse plateau, its light stone buildings cling to the hillside rising irregularly to the summit which is crowned by a Renaissance château.

Excursions from here include the road through the hills to **Sénanque**, the stone bories at the **Village des Bories** (*see* page 63), the small Romansque church in **Saint-Pantaléon** (a tiny temple to Christianity with primitive tombs), and the lavender fields beyond. An interesting museum, **La Musée de Lavande**, at Coustellet explains the extraction process.

Above: *The Abbey at Sénanque is one of the best-restored Cistercian abbeys in France.*

Sénanque ★★★

The **Abbaye Notre-Dame de Sénanque** (open daily, morning and afternoon), a picturesque 12th-century Cistercian building, rises – for one glorious month each year – above a velvety swathe of purple lavender. Founded in 1148, the austere order chose a perfect location for their abbey. Although it suffered from various attacks, notably the 16th-century insurrection of the heretic Vaudois, it is today in a fine state of repair thanks to the benevolence of later buyers, and still active.

Its clean lines are in perfect harmony with the beliefs of the order. The church is unusually oriented in that the apse and altar face north. Note the attractive cloister, central to Abbey life, and the ingenious cupola in the four corners of the transept, which bridges the corners between vaults. As this is a major attraction, the Abbey can get crowded and an early or late visit is recommended.

FURTHER AFIELD

Two small towns worth a short detour are **Ansouis** and **La Tour d'Aigues**. Ansouis houses the **Château d'Ansouis** (open to visitors), owned by the same family for some 700 years. La Tour d'Aigues has the remains of what must once have been a beautiful Renaissance palace.

> ### THE CISTERCIANS
>
> There are three exceptional Cistercian buildings In Provence: Silvacane, Sénanque and the Abbey of Le Thoronet. Their history dates back to the early 12th century. Tired with the increasing wealth and power of the Church, **Robert de Molesme** decided to return to a strict interpretation of the 6th-century **rule of Saint Benedict** which espoused poverty, humility, obedience, and a balance between prayer and labour. He founded a monastery in 1098 at Cîteaux, after which four 'daughter-houses' were established at **Clairvaux**, Ferté, Morimond and Pontigny. It was Clairvaux which became the centre of the order under **Saint Bernard** and from there monasteries were founded throughout Europe. By 1134, there were already 74 abbeys, and by the turn of the century they had grown to 125.

Vaucluse at a Glance

BEST TIMES TO VISIT

Any time is good in this part of Provence. City hotels remain open all year while some (not all) *chambres d'hôte* also remain open. **Winters** can be cold, especially if the mistral blows in the Rhône valley. Mountains are often snow-capped though it's rare to have snow in the towns. **Summers** are invariably hot and crowded, while **spring** and **autumn** are mellow. The lavender and lavandin are at their best in July. Most festivals are from Easter to September. The **Avignon Festival** runs from the second week to end July; Avignon's **Marché de Noël** runs from 11–31 December.

GETTING THERE

The nearest major airport to Vaucluse is **Marseille**, 100km (62 miles) away. Avignon is located just off the toll-paying A7 motorway which heads north to Montélimar and Paris (685km or 428 miles), south to Marseille and on to Nice (260km or 162 miles). Good *routes nationales* and well-maintained *routes départementales* mean that all sights are easily accessible by car. **Buses** link Avignon with Paris, Marseille and Nice. For information contact the Gare Routière, the bus station, tel: 04 90 82 07 35. Avignon is also on one of France's main **railway lines** and fast connections lead to Paris and Montpellier (both high-speed

TGV services), west to Spain, and southeast to Marseille and Nice. For all railway information tel: 08 36 35 35 35, or for English-language operators, 08 36 35 35 39.

GETTING AROUND

All towns in Vaucluse are small enough to explore on foot. **Taxis** are available, but not cheap. For travel between towns and villages there are some local **bus** services linking villages to their nearest towns though the frequency may not be more than once daily. Check at the tourist offices in each town for the schedules. The easiest way is to hire a car and explore the area yourself.

WHERE TO STAY

LUXURY
Hôtel de la Mirande,
place de la Mirande, Avignon, tel: 04 90 85 93 93,
fax: 90 86 26 85, website:
http://www.la-mirande.fr
Intimate, supremely elegant hotel. Excellent restaurant.
Hostellerie Crillon le Brave,
place de l'Église, Crillon-le-Brave, tel: 04 90 65 61 61,
fax: 90 65 62 86, e-mail:
crillonbrave@relaischateaux.fr
Provençal hotel in medieval village. Excellent restaurant.
Hostellerie Le Phébus,
Joucas, Gordes, tel: 04 90 05 78 83, fax: 90 05 73 61,
e-mail: XMathieu@aol.com
Converted *bastide* (country house). Elegant rooms, some with private pools.

MID-RANGE
Hostellerie Château des Fines Roches, Châteauneuf-du-Pape, tel: 04 90 83 70 23,
fax: 90 83 78 42, website:
www.chateauneuf-du-pape.
enprovence.com/finesroches
A delightful hotel overlooking vineyards near Châteauneuf.
Mas de la Sénancole, les Imberts, Gordes, tel: 04 90 76 76 55, fax: 90 76 70 44.
Spacious and peaceful hotel, pleasant garden and pool.

BUDGET
La Garance, Ste-Colombe, near Bédoin, tel: 04 90 12 81 00, fax: 90 65 93 05. Semi-rural hotel with pool, ideal for exploring Mont Ventoux.
Le Renaissance, place du Château, Gordes, tel: 04 90 72 02 02, fax: 90 72 05 11.
Very small, welcoming hotel situated within castle walls. Booking is essential.
Le Mas de la tour, Gargas, Roussillon, tel: 04 90 74 12 10, fax: 90 04 83 67. An extended *mas* with restaurant and swimming pool.

WHERE TO EAT

LUXURY
Hôtel de la Mirande,
Avignon (*see* Where to Stay).
Old-world charm in fine setting. Excellent wine list.
Christian Étienne,
10 rue Mons, Avignon,
tel: 04 90 86 16 50. Very popular, highly rated restaurant next to Palace. Reservations recommended.

Vaucluse at a Glance

Hostellerie Le Phébus, Joucas, (see Where to Stay). Fine terrace restaurant with panoramic views towards Luberon. Innovative cuisine.
Les Terrasses, La Bastide de Gordes, Gordes, tel: 04 90 72 12 12. An unmatchable view westwards from Gordes. Offering fine cuisine.

MID-RANGE

Moulin à Huile, quai Mar Foch, Vaison-la-Romaine, tel: 04 90 36 20 67. Innovative cuisine with Provençal roots, in a fine old mill.
Saule Pleureur, route de Avignon, Monteux (near Carpentras), tel: 04 90 62 01 35. Renowned restaurant with good Provençal cuisine. Reservations recommended, especially at weekends.
Hostellerie Crillon le Brave (see Where to Stay). Excellent meals in a superb setting. Reservations essential.
Auberge du Luberon, 17 quai Léon Sagy, Apt, tel: 04 90 74 12 50. Highly rated, reservations essential. Also has some inexpensive rooms.

BUDGET

La Cuisine de Reine, le Cloître des Arts, 83 rue Joseph Vernet, Avignon, tel: 04 90 85 99 04. Pleasant airy cloister setting for excellent Provençal cuisine, good value.
La Garbure, 3 rue Joseph Ducos, Châteauneuf-du-Pape, tel: 04 90 83 75 08, fax: 04 90 83 52 34. Small hotel-

restaurant run by an ebullient chef; has an excellent reputation and offers good wines.
Lou Fanau, Fontaine-de-Vaucluse, tel: 04 90 20 20 11. Popular spot, especially in the summer months.
Le Carré aux Herbes, Le Carré de l'Isle, Isle-sur-la-Sorgue, tel: 04 90 38 62 95. Excellent restaurant where you are quite likely to rub shoulders with antique-hunting celebrities.
Hostellerie Provençale, place du Château, Gordes, tel: 04 90 72 10 01. Popular central eatery opposite castle, with pizzas, grills and ices.

SHOPPING

The is a good area to buy traditional Provençal produce. Fabrics, linen and household goods can be found in the many markets and also in Avignon. Local markets are a source of handicrafts, food products, pottery and Provençal herbs. Don't miss buying select Rhône wines and, in particular, those from Châteauneuf-du-Pape, among the world's finest.
Léopold, place du Change, Avignon, tel: 04 90 82 72 95,

has a fine collection of Provençal fabric and linen.

USEFUL CONTACTS

Office de tourisme, 41 cours J-Jaurès, Avignon, tel: 04 32 74 32 74.
Office de tourisme, cours A-Briand, Orange, tel: 04 90 34 70 88.
Office de tourisme, place Albert I, Uzès, tel: 04 66 22 68 88.
Office de tourisme, place Chanoine Sautel, Vaison-la-Romaine, tel: 04 90 36 02 11.
Office de tourisme, place Église, Isle-sur-la-Sorgue, tel: 04 90 38 04 78.
Cap Canoe, route de Barjac, St-Ambroix, tel: 04 66 24 25 16. Hires out canoes and kayaks in the Cèze valley. All levels of experience.
Cristallerie des Papes, Fontaine-de-Vaucluse, tel: 04 90 20 32 52. Master glass-blowers. Fine range of lamps, vases, paperweights, and artistic creations.
Montgolfière Provence Ballooning, Joucas, Gordes, tel: 04 90 05 76 77, fax: 90 05 74 39. Morning balloon flights over the Luberon valley. Booking essential.

AVIGNON	J	F	M	A	M	J	J	A	S	O	N	D
AVERAGE TEMP. °F	41	44	50	56	62	70	74	73	67	58	48	43
AVERAGE TEMP. °C	5	6	10	13	16	20	23	22	19	14	9	6
HOURS OF SUN DAILY	3	4	6	6	7	9	9	8	7	5	4	3
RAINFALL in	0.8	1.2	1.6	1.9	2.4	1.6	1.2	1.6	2.4	3.1	2.8	1.9
RAINFALL mm	20	30	40	50	60	40	30	40	60	80	70	50

4
Les Alpes de Haute-Provence

This area is one of the most scenic parts of France and in total contrast to the better known areas of Provence around Arles, Aix-en-Provence or Marseille. Rugged terrain, snow-capped mountain peaks and extraordinary geological formations characterize the varied landscape. Indeed, there are sections of mountain-side that look as if they were flung out of the earth, folded, pulled apart and then refolded, such are the complex sandwiched striations.

Haute-Provence is decidedly alpine in nature – it is one of France's **winter sports** playgrounds and embraces both impressive peaks and verdant valleys. Favourite skiing destinations include Isola 2000, the Val d'Allos, Annot-Allons and the resorts around Barcelonnette.

Within these confines there are vast protected reserves, including the **Parc National du Mercantour** and the massive **Réserve Géologique de Haute-Provence** which teems with **fossils** and **ammonites**. The inhabitants of this region have a respect for nature, and small mammals and alpine birds thrive, while the **flora** is allowed to proliferate almost without refrain. It is a botanist's dream. Another impressive feature is the series of deep gorges, the **Gorges du Verdon**, one of Europe's most breathtaking canyons.

This is also a region known since antiquity for its thermal baths, such as those at **Digne-les-Bains** and **Gréoux les-Bains**. It was a decisive strategic outpost for **Napoleon** who passed through in 1815 on his return journey from exile in Elba.

DON'T MISS

*** Gorges du Verdon: breathtaking canyons.
*** Parc National du Mercantour: a beautiful national park.
** Le Petit Train: from Digne-les-Bains to Nice.
** Lavender fields: near the town of Valensole.
** Moustiers-Sainte-Marie: great for ceramics.
* Sisteron: a lively, old perched town.
* Entrevaux: strategic medieval town.

Opposite: *After its spectacular gorges, the River Verdon flows into Lake Sainte-Croix.*

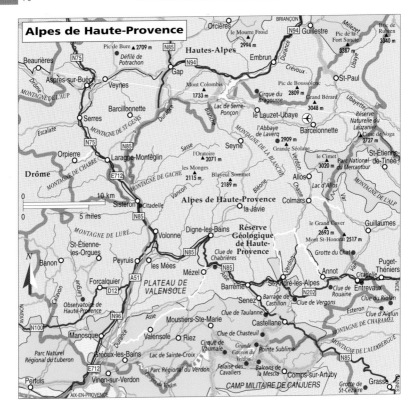

WESTERN HAUTE-PROVENCE
Digne-les-Bains ★★

Capital of the *département* Haute-Provence, this elegant spa town is the self-styled capital of the lavender region. The Romans discovered the therapeutic value of the waters which surface from two springs at a temperature of 29°C–49°C (85°F–120°F) and contain a substantial quantity of minerals such as chlorine, sulphur and sodium. They are highly reputed for treating rheumatism and respiratory problems. **Les Thermes** is just 4km (2.5 miles) from the centre of Digne and offers visitors the chance to stay in local hotels for a prolonged visit, or enjoy (by appointment) a day's treatment.

The philosopher and mathematician, **Pierre Gassendi**, was the town's most notable son, and one soon realizes this as streets and buildings are named after him. This 16th-century sage is also honoured with a statue in the **place Général de Gaulle**. The **Musée Municipal** (64 bd Gassendi, tel: 04 92 31 45 29, re-opening mid 2002) displays Pierre Gassendi's scientific instruments along with a number of 18th- and 19th-century European paintings.

Of architectural interest is the **Notre-Dame-du-Bourg**, a large Romanesque church started in the 12th century. Note its fine portal. Lovers of flowers shouldn't miss the **Jardin Botanique** (Couvent des Cordeliers, opposite the Musée Municipal, open Tuesday to Saturday, morning and afternoon, April to end October). It houses some 350 species of plants, all local, and is particularly pleasant as it is contained within the convent walls.

Petit Train des Pignes **

On Sundays during the summer months, the *Chemins de Fer de Provence* run a small train service between Digne-les-Bains and Nice. The *Petit Train* is pulled by a steam locomotive for part of the 3-hour journey and by diesel engine for the rest. However, during the week there is an identical diesel service four times daily in each direction.

Between the palm-fringed coast of the Côte d'Azur and the cool heights of Haute-Provence, the train follows a magnificent route via small towns and amid wild, uninhabited scenery, passing through 25 tunnels and over some 30 viaducts and bridges. It takes you to the towns of Puget, Théniers, Annot, Saint-André-les-Alpes and Entrevaux. If you catch the earliest train of the day it is possible to stop twice en route and return on the last train, 13 hours later.

> **THE LAVENDER TRAIL**
>
> Lavender is celebrated with particular verve during the month of August. Lavender lovers can, however, enjoy this flower at other times of the year too. The plant is in bloom from late June till August and the best sights are on the Valensole plateau, the Vallée de l'Asse and des Duyes, around Mézel and Camptercier. At Coustellet (on the Route de Gordes) the **Musée de la Lavande**, tel: 04 90 76 91 23 will walk you through the copper stills through which the lavender oils are distilled, show a short film and teach you how the industry is run in modern times. You can also try the lavender cures at one of the spas. Digne's **Les Thermes**, tel: 04 92 32 32 32 offers the *bain lavande*, a mixture of mineral waters and oil of lavender administered in a jacuzzi-style bath.

Below: *The Penitents, near les Mées – rocks with an interesting legend.*

Below: *Capital of a mountainous region, Sisteron has a notable 13th-century citadel.*

Réserve Géologique de Haute-Provence ★

This reserve encompasses 1900km² (734 sq miles) and was created to preserve the many ammonites and fossils for which this area is known. Here 300 million years of history is being conserved and to learn more about it, visit the **Réserve Géologique de Haute-Provence Musée** (Parc Saint-Benoît, open weekdays, morning and afternoon). The museum is divided into six zones, each offering an introduction to different aspects of our earth. The multimedia presentation on regional geology, the extraordinary collection of fossils and the aquariums, both stocked with tropical and Mediterranean species, are excellent.

Sisteron ★

Sisteron lay about halfway in Napoleon's forced march between Golfe-Juan and Grenoble in 1815. He arrived here on Wednesday 1 March, and was welcomed by the mayor, not by royalist opposition. He had a meal at the **Auberge du Bras d'Or** (still run by a relative of the original owners who served Napoleon), and forged on northwards.

Like Napoleon, the first thing one sees on arriving near Sisteron is her superb, 13th-century citadel dominating not just the old town but the whole Durance valley. In the summer, the Citadel hosts **Les Nuits du Citadelle**, a season of open-air ballet and theatre which attracts some fine international performers. Perhaps it's wishful thinking to call Sisteron 'the Pearl of Upper Provence' but, like a pearl, you need to give it a little time and consideration to be able to appreciate its appeal. Don't miss a look at the 12th-century **Église Notre-Dame**, a fine Romanesque building. Wander through the slim alleys of the **Vieille Ville** and tour around the **citadel** but try to take a moment to gaze out over the valley of the Durance and marvel at its spectacular site.

Saint-André-les-Alpes ★

This town sits at a crossroads where the rivers Verdon and Moriez meet, and makes a good base from which to explore the region. The lakes **de Castillon** and **d'Allos** are just a few kilometres away, the **d'Allos Pass** is 45 minutes by road, and the spectacular part of the **Gorges du Verdon** a similar distance. Hikers, ramblers, botanists, anglers, windsurfers, canoeists and cyclists can all indulge in their pastimes here. Come July and cyclists will have a chance of seeing the *Tour de France*, Europe's premier cycling race, pass through the valley between Allos and Saint-André.

Above: *Lake Castillon affords ramblers some superb natural scenery.*

Valensole is lavender land. In midsummer the rows of lavender compete with the golden expanses of wheat. It is here, on this plateau, that France's greatest concentration of lavender and lavandin (*see* panel) is grown.

Southern Area

This area is one of spiky hills and rocky outcrops where small villages at strategic points bore witness to centuries of turbulent history.

Gorges du Verdon ★★★

These magnificent gorges are worth exploring over several days. Despite their age, it was less than 100 years ago that they were really discovered and explored. Slicing a great vertical abyss, sometimes as deep as 700m (2300ft) from top to bottom, the gorges provide some excellent venues for hikers, nature lovers and watersports enthusiasts – whitewater rafting and canoeing have become very popular along the lower reaches of the gorge, while kayaking is possible up the river in the turquoise waters of **Lac de Sainte-Croix**. But look up too. Seeing the gorges from micro- and ultralights is a popular pastime, as are rock climbing and sky diving. Terrestial nature lovers will find

---

LAVENDER OR LAVANDIN?

The gently mauve sways of lavender (*Lavandula angustifolia*) are a beautiful summer sight in Provence. The fragrance and oil that lavender gives has been used for millennia in perfumes, medicine and for storage. It is grown on the Vaucluse and Valensole plains at an altitude of between 400m and 1100m (1300–3500ft). To produce 1kg (2.2lb) of lavender oil essence, some 130kg (287lb) of flowers are required, so a hybrid variety, lavandin, has been created from a cross between lavender and aspic (*Lavandula latifolia*) from which only 40kg (88lb) of flowers are needed to yield 1kg (2.2lb) of oil. But the purists argue that the quality of this oil is not good enough for perfume. It is destined for pharmaceutical and industrial perfumes, such as those used in cleaning products.

Right: *The lake of Sainte-Croix fills with the waters of the Verdon and has become a popular place for watersports.*

that the area is particularly rich in flora and fauna – the topography and the fact that this is a reserve contribute much to the attractiveness of the area.

Those who wish to explore the landscape from the top and take in one panorama after another can opt for a circular route which follows the ridges on either side. It is neither a fast nor an easy drive, for the road is narrow and winding, but there are dozens of viewpoints from which the Gorges du Verdon may be viewed.

Castellane *

Like the points of the compass, four national roads meet at Castellane and, presiding over the town, visible for kilometres around, is the church and steeple of the Baroque **Notre-Dame-du-Roc**. The town is a pretty spot straddling the River Verdon, and one of the major places for exploring the Gorges du Verdon. Although its history goes back centuries there are few tangible reminders of its medieval past.

Annot *

This small, sunny town at the bottom of the Vaire valley is known for its **troglodyte houses**. Originally there were quite a few homes hewn out of the local sandstone, but due to modern methods of earthmoving few have survived the decades. However, on the northern side of town, in a back alley on the way to the Chapelle, you

---

TROGLODYTE DWELLINGS

There are a number of troglodyte homes in Provence. Built both for safety and for insulation from the elements, they survive as an oddity in the 21st century. Annot still has a few of these homes which are occupied. There are also interesting cave homes in Villecroze, and the château at Les-Baux-de-Provence has some further remains.

can still see some of the houses that were created around the huge rock blocks known as *grès*. The old part of Annot, around the rue **Notre-Dame** and the **Grand Rue**, has some interesting architectural details. Its narrow streets and deep shadows are particularly evocative of medieval times. Annot is also on the **Petit Train de Pignes** railway route.

Entrevaux *

Its name translates as 'between valleys' and, indeed, this small walled town lies at the meeting of two valleys. But it is the extraordinary fortress which demands your attention, for atop a rocky outcrop, a tiring 20-minute hike from the town centre and linked to the town by zigzagging walls that seem to match those of China's Great Wall, lies a fortified citadel, the achievement of Louis XIV's military architect and engineer, Vauban.

Another architectural gem in Entrevaux is the **cathedral** with its beautifully carved walnut doors. And while you're looking at buildings, don't miss the **old mills** – an oil mill (you will notice that Entrevaux has plenty of olive terraces in the area) and a flour mill. Interestingly, Entrevaux was – until 1860 – a town on the France–Savoie border. Still today it has a **Porte de France** and a **Porte d'Italie**.

MEDIEVAL FESTIVITIES

The towns in the eastern part of this region have variously been under German and Italian (Savoy) rule and French domination. Because of their relative isolation, they have retained many of their old traditions. **Colmars** is known for its costumed Fêtes Médiévales in the second week of August; **Castellane** is proud of its Fête des Pétardiers (31 January) which dates back to a 1586 victory in the War of the Religions; and **Entrevaux** celebrates its own **Fêtes Médiévales**, biennial in August with costumed crusaders.

Below: *Medieval traditions are relived with Entrevaux's annual Fêtes Médiévales each August.*

Below: *Examples of traditional faïence from Moustiers-Sainte-Marie.*

Moustiers-Sainte-Marie ★★

Clinging to the western face of the craggy peaks on a limestone mountainside, Moustiers-Sainte-Marie has a reputation for some of France's finest **faïence**. As you arrive at Moustiers, one of the first things you'll notice is the gleaming **star** which hangs suspended above the town. Legend has it that this is the plaque given by a knight in thanks for a safe homecoming from the crusades. Just below the town lies the **Chapelle Notre-Dame de Beauvoir**, accessible by a winding path.

It was during the 17th and 18th centuries that Moustiers' faïence achieved world renown. The delicate designs, often portraying birds, animals and natural scenes on a white background, are most distinctive. Its popularity with the aristocracy lasted some 200 years until the fashion for English porcelain displaced it and the industry subsided. Today the craft has been rekindled and a score of **pottery workshops** is active producing tableware, ornaments, lamps and other household items. There are various qualities on offer (to suit a variety of purses) and the differences soon become evident. Three ateliers are open, mornings only, for public visits.

The best way to discover Moustiers is to wander slowly (the town is more like a village) through its narrow streets and past the many shops and restaurants. It gets very full during summer when it is advisable to park at the outskirts of Moustiers and walk into the centre. If you plan a visit in autumn, note that on 31 August and 8 September local **processions** take place.

NORTHERN HAUTE-PROVENCE

The area to the north of Digne-les-Bains is picturesquely alpine and has more in common, both geographically and climatically, with Italy or its more northern neighbour Switzerland than it does with the southern stretches of Provence.

Barcelonnette *

The singularity of this northern-most town lies in the fact that it has a number of **Mexican villas**. Although a little incongruous, these elaborate homes were built by local factory owners (such as the **Arnaud brothers**) who, with failing bank balances in the fabric business, took off to Mexico where they made their

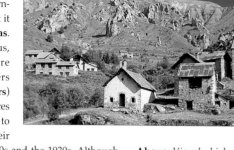

Above: *Vignols, high in the Mercantour National Park.*

fortunes between the late 1880s and the 1930s. Although these rich edifices were the product of Mexican profit, their design owes much to Tyrolean, Italian and Baroque architecture. The Mexican link is further cemented in the **place Manuel** with its beautiful fountain.

The three-storey **Villa Sapinère** (10 av de la Libération, open Wednesday, Thursday and Saturday afternoon) offers an interesting small museum with the history of the Arnaud brothers' Mexican sojourn, costumes and printed material. It also offers temporary exhibitions. Located on the ground floor is the **Maison du Parc National du Mercantour** where you can get information about this important French national park.

Parc National du Mercantour ***

Together with the island of Port-Cros off the southern coast, this northern park constitutes one of only two French national parks found in Provence.

Rising to a height of 3143m (10,312ft) at Cime du Gélas and encompassing an unusual **geological formation** of countless folded limestone layers, deep gorges and jagged peaks, this is a fascinating wilderness zone which, since 1979, has been a protected area. It is unusual, in that it is sandwiched between the Mediterranean and Alps, two very different climatic and geological zones. The park is divided into two sections: the first (peripheral) where village activity in harmony with nature is allowed, and the second (central) which is dedicated entirely to the protection of its biological diversity.

The national park has over 600km (375 miles) of marked **hiking trails**, some of which offer information panels for identification of species. Botanists should look out for some of the 2000 species of plants, of which 200 are rare and 30 endemic.

Colmars *

This little village (with its tiny streets, small squares, tumbling fountains and ancient stone houses who could fail to fall under its charm?) is contained between two medieval forts and placed in a wonderfully wooded mountain landscape. It was once a border post between France and the territory of the Duke of Savoy, and its ramparts were continually upgraded right into the 18th century. Its history, however, goes back to Roman times, when a temple to Mars was erected here.

Like Barcelonnette, Colmars is an ideal place from which nature lovers can explore the scenic lakes, rivers and mountains of the surrounding countryside. Located just above the **River Verdon**, Colmars is actually in the most northerly part of the **Parc Régional du Verdon** which passes through the crossroads town of **Saint-André-les-Alpes**. Continuing further southwards through the **Lac de Castillon**, the park envelopes the fabulous Gorges du Verdon (*see* page 73) coming out into the **Lac de Sainte-Croix**.

Right: *The European marmot, frequently sighted during summer in the Mercantour National Park.*

Les Alpes de Haute-Provence at a Glance

BEST TIMES TO VISIT

Winter sports enthusiasts head for this area from **November** until **Easter**. The ski slopes and après-ski activities are excellent during this period. Late spring is best for botanists and ornithologists, while holidaymakers find the area at its most enjoyable from **June** to **September**.

GETTING THERE

This area is bordered by the high Alps in the east and the River Durance in the west. The A51 runs from Marseille to Sisteron, the N85 from Cannes to Digne, following the historic Route Napoleon. Trains run from the south.

GETTING AROUND

Within the area, the easiest way to travel is by car.

WHERE TO STAY

LUXURY

La Bastide de Moustiers, chemin de Quinson, Moustiers-Ste-Marie, tel: 04 92 70 47 47, fax: 92 70 47 48, e-mail: bastide@i2m.fr
A beautifully restored country house just 1.5km (1 mile) outside town. Only 11 rooms and an excellent restaurant.
La Bonne Étape, chemin du lac, Château-Arnoux, tel: 04 92 64 00 09, fax: 92 64 37 36, e-mail: bonneetape @relaixchateaux.fr
Select and Provençal. Midway between Haute-Provence and Luberon. Excellent restaurant.

MID-RANGE

Grand Paris 19 bd Thiers, Digne-les-Bains, tel: 04 92 31 11 15, fax: 92 32 32 82. Digne' best address, just a couple of minutes' walk from the town centre. Good restaurant.
La Crémaillère, route de Riez, Gréoux-les-Bains, tel: 04 92 70 40 04, fax: 92 78 19 80. A mid-sized hotel with a pleasant personal feel. A converted farmhouse with traditional Provençal decor. Good restaurant.
Les Gorges du Verdon, La Palud-sur-Verdon, tel: 04 92 77 38 26, fax: 92 77 35 00. Modern, medium-sized hotel near the northern edge of the gorge. Pleasant restaurant.
Azteca, rue des Trois-Frères-Arnaud, tel 04 92 81 46 36, fax: 92 81 43 92. A Mexican villa in the tradition of this town. Has 27 rooms, much favoured during the skiing season. Small restaurant.

BUDGET

Le Clair Logis, route de Digne, St-André-les-Alpes, tel: 04 922 89 19 36, fax: 04 92 89 19 30. Small, family-run hotel in a good location to explore the region. Good restaurant.
Auberge du Teillon, route Napoléon, La Garde, Castellane, tel: 04 92 83 60 88, fax: 04 92 83 74 08. Just outside Castellane, a pleasant small hotel with restaurant (closed in winter).

WHERE TO EAT

LUXURY TO MID-RANGE

Les Santons, place de l'Église, Moustiers-Ste-Marie, tel: 04 92 74 66 48. Good views over the valley. This restaurant offers fine Provençal cuisine.
La Bastide de Moustiers (*see* Where to Stay). The restaurant is owned by award-winning chef, Alain Ducasse. Cuisine reflects local produce. Excellent wine list.
La Bonne Étape (*see* Where to Stay). A good place for excellent local Provençal cuisine, reflecting locally produced ingredients.

MID-RANGE TO BUDGET

Grand Paris (*see* Where to Stay). North and south Provence mix in this cuisine.

USEFUL CONTACTS

Office de tourisme, place du Tampinet, Digne-les-Bains, tel: 04 92 36 62 62.
Office de tourisme, Hôtel-de-Ville, Sisteron, tel: 04 92 61 04 51.
Office de tourisme, Hôtel-Dieu, Moustiers-Ste-Marie, tel: 04 92 73 67 84.
Office de tourisme, place Frédéric Mistral, Barcelonnette, tel: 04 92 81 04 71.
Établissement Thermal de Digne-les-Bains, tel: 04 92 32 32 32, fax: 04 92 32 38 15, e-mail: thermes_digne@wanadoo.fr
Reservations for individual or a range of treatments.

5
The Côte d'Azur and Alpes Maritimes

This beautiful part of France was known, well beyond its present national boundaries, long before tourists set foot along the shores of the French Mediterranean. The Greeks stopped here on their way to Massalia (Marseille) and Iberica (Spain); the Romans enjoyed a change from duties in the capital in their Provincia, and Impressionist artists seeking inspiration came here from all parts of Europe. Today's traveller is just one more in a long line of people enjoying the beauty of southern France.

The sea along the Azure Coast (the name was coined in the 19th century) is indeed blue in the limpid days of summer. The small bays and sandy shoreline between the main cities, **Cannes**, **Nice**, **Monte-Carlo** and **Menton**, attract numerous holidaymakers while the resorts, forever smartening up their façades and polishing their cultural legacy, offer all the facilities of the grander European cities.

Among these cosmopolitan centres, small towns, *villages perchés* and tiny stone villages paint a pretty picture as they curve around the indented coast, or stand out in an impressive, often breathtaking, landscape.

The Alpes Maritimes form a fine backdrop to the shore and hide within their valleys centuries of history shared by the French and Italians. The principality of Monaco, small but important, continues to retrieve land from the sea to increase its size and potential.

Like the artists who chose to paint the beauty of this area and who have left an unparalleled artistic legacy in the region's museums, today's tourist will find far more than he ever imagined to occupy his time here.

DON'T MISS

*** **Musée Matisse:** Nice.
*** **Les Corniches**, spectacular coastal drive.
*** **Éze:** a picturesque and dramatic perched village.
*** **Monaco:** impressive – especially by night.
** **Menton:** known for its flowers and lemons.
** **Chapelle du Rosaire:** Matisse-designed chapel located in Vence.
** **Grasse:** an afternoon among the perfumes.
* **Promenade des Anglais:** for an evening stroll.

Opposite: *The fabulous floating wealth of Monaco's Yacht Marina.*

NICE

The largest city on the French Mediterranean coast, Nice occupies a sheltered position between the glittering **Baie des Anges** and the pre-Alps. It was settled by Romans in 154BC, who founded the town **Cemenelum** (Cimiez). Since its early days, Nice has had a turbulent history, being incorporated into France only in 1860. Its mild climate and impressive Riviera setting attracted many artists and vast numbers of wealthy Europeans (many of them English) during the *belle époque*. The famous epithet, Côte d'Azur, was coined at this time.

La Vieille Ville ★★★

The old town, heart of traditional Nice, is a warren of narrow streets echoing with a life of its own, an area where the Niçois live and one to which tourists are inevitably drawn. Some of the ochre-coloured buildings are decorated with painted friezes, sculpted elements and unusual trompe l'œil designs emulating grander buildings elsewhere. Over 170 façades have been carefully restored. At its southern edge lies the renovated **Cours Saleya**, site of the much-photographed daily vegetable and flower market, and now a trendy place to lunch or stop for a drink.

In the midst of this old quartier lies the **Cathédrale Sainte-Réparate**, a stately Baroque building with a glistening tiled dome built in 1650. The **Palais Lascaris** (located at 15 rue Droite, open Tuesday to Sunday, December to October), a beautiful 17th-century palace and the finest aristocratic residence in Nice, has an interesting grand staircase, tapestries and sculpture. A couple of churches in the Vieille Ville also merit a visit. These include the **Église Saint-Martin-Saint-Augustin** and **Église Saint-Jacques**.

Musée d'Art Moderne et d'Art Contemporain ★★

At the northern end of the old town, the wide area of **boulevard Jean Jaurès** meets place Garibaldi. Opposite lies the striking modern glass-and-marble **Musée d'Art Moderne et d'Art Contemporain**, MAMAC (Promenade

Opposite: *A modern building, constructed to hold Nice's Musée d'Art Moderne et d'Art Contemporain.*

des Arts, open daily except Tuesday). Housed on three floors are works dating from the second half of the 20th century. The artists featured are, in many instances, still active: there are paintings by, among others, Andy Warhol, Yves Klein, Roy Lichtenstein, César Baldacchini, Christo Javacheff, Tom Wesselmann and Claes Oldenbourg.

The Port *

Protected by a modern jetty and sheltering in the shadow of the **Château**, this deep-set port is one of Nice's most attractive features for the light dances of its yachts and luxury pleasure **cruisers**, offset by the warm ochres and siennas of some of its gracious older buildings lining the harbour. From here, there are regular **ferry crossings** to Corsica. Behind, in the *quartier* Ségurane, lie the numerous **antique shops** much beloved by bargain seekers.

CIMIEZ AREA

This area to the north was the site of the original Roman town of **Cemenelum**. It has some vestiges of the pre-Christian era, two exceptionally interesting museums, scores of elegant homes and the ultra-gracious *belle époque* **Hôtel Regina**.

Musée Marc Chagall **

This museum (av du Docteur Ménard, open daily except Tuesday) is dedicated to the œuvre of Russian emigré, Marc Chagall (1887–1985), who worked in Paris and the south of France during much of the 20th century. Among the highlights are the exhibition of his whimsical stained-glass windows, naive yet colourful paintings and the mosaic which the artist created for this museum. There is also an interesting collection of lithographs, engravings, gouaches and books.

LA CUISINE NIÇOISE

It is said that there are more three-star restaurants per square metre in Nice than anywhere else in France. The mixture of Mediterranean ingredients, France's famous Provençal *primeurs*, the proximity to Italy and an often wealthy clientele have all done much to create competition among local *cuisiniers*. Nice is also the only town to have an AOC wine, the **Bellet**, which is available in red, white or rosé. Among the town's most notable creations are the *pissaladière*, a flat, pizza-like dough dressed with anchovies, tomato paste, olives etcetera; *socca*, pancakes made from chickpeas; *pan-bagnat*, Nice's answer to a doughnut; *ratatouille*, a courgette and vegetable stew; courgette flower fritters; stuffed vegetables and, of course, *salade niçoise*, a lettuce, green bean, tuna, egg and olive salad.

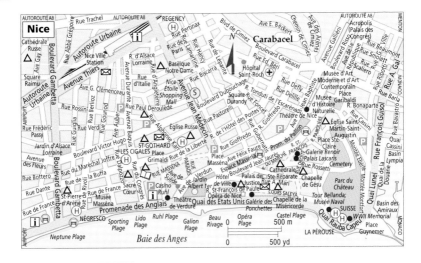

Musée Matisse ★★★

This is one of France's greatest museums (av des Arènes de Cimiez, open daily except Tuesday). In the burgundy-red Villa des Arènes, a 17th-century Genoese villa with a trompe l'œil façade, are displayed some of **Henri Matisse's** works. Matisse (1869–1954) lived in the city, not far from the site of this museum, from 1917 until his death. This museum traces his œuvre and the influence he had on contemporaries. There are gouaches, sculptures and drawings (including sketches for the Chapelle du Rosaire at Vence, *see* page 94). Some of the notable paintings include the pointillist *Femme à ombrelle* (1905), *Odalisque au coffret rouge* (1926) and the striking *Fauteuil rocaille* (1946). Look out for his paper cut-outs such as the lovely blue *Nu bleu IV* created in 1952 or his *Baigneuse dans les roseaux* done in the same year, both fashioned late in life when he was no longer able to paint.

The **Musée archéologique**, contained in the same building as the Musée Matisse, documents the early history of Nice, while the 17th-century **Monastère de Cimiez** houses a free museum illustrating **Franciscan** life from the 18th century to the current day.

ALONG THE BAIE DES ANGES

The Bay of Angels provides Nice with its gentle breezes and clean air. It was here that most of the elegant 19th- and 20th-century *belle époque* buildings were constructed.

Promenade des Anglais ★★

It was the 19th-century English community which paid for this signature promenade – a 5km-long (3-mile), broad avenue dressed with palm trees and wide pavements following the curve of the pebbly shore. It is the lungs of Nice, a gathering and strolling place, and the gallery for watching Nice's bathers and sunworshippers. On its southern end lies the *belle époque* **Hôtel Négresco**, another Nice landmark. Built in 1912 for Henri Négresco, it has hosted royalty and glitterati for most of its life and still remains its most prestigious address.

Musée Masséna ★

The Museum of Art and History, situated just behind the Négresco (65 rue de France and 35 Promenade des Anglais, open daily morning and afternoon, except Monday), is in an elegant 19th-century Italianate villa that houses an important collection of artifacts relating to the history of Nice and its earldom from the 11th to the 19th century. There is a good collection of sacred art, arms and armoury, Mediterranean ceramics and an art gallery of paintings by local 19th- and early 20th-century artists.

Musée de Beaux Arts ★★

Nice's Fine Arts Museum is appropriately housed in a fine 19th-century villa (which was built for a Ukrainian princess). It displays a good collection of 17th-century Italian paintings, as well as some excellent 18th-century French works (keep a lookout especially for the

Below: *The Promenade des Anglais defines the shoreline of Nice.*

MUSÉE EPHRUSSI DE ROTHSCHILD

Highlight of Cap-Ferrat is the **Musée Ephrussi de Rothschild** (open daily from 10:00), a wonderfully grandiose villa crowning the summit of the cape, constructed in an Italianate fashion for the somewhat unusual Baroness Béatrice Ephrussi, née Rothschild (1864–1934). Little of the interior is accessible, though some of the private rooms occupied by the baroness are (do admire the collection of porcelain in the dining room). But it is the **seven gardens**, each with their own distinct style, that captivate. Waterfalls, Roman-style sculpture, shady walks and brilliant stands of flowers take you through **Florentine**, **French** and **Spanish** gardens, to exotic and rose gardens.

Fragonard canvasses) and a commendable collection of 19th-century work, including some **Impressionist** and **Post-Impressions** works.

LES CORNICHES

Three superb routes fan out from Nice towards the Italian border. Respectively known as the **Grande Corniche** (the highest of the three roads), the **Moyenne Corniche**, (a mid-level road) and the **Basse Corniche** (following the coastline), they thread some beautiful and popular towns and villages, and often afford stunning vistas of the Mediterranean coast.

Saint-Jean-Cap-Ferrat ★★★

Taking the Basse Corniche, Saint-Jean-Cap-Ferrat (often referred to only by the name of this gorgeous cape, Cap Ferrat), is just 10 minutes from Nice. Within the fragrant pine forests that clad the whole small peninsula nestle opulent residences and luxury villas: Cap Ferrat welcomes discreet wealth. The village of **Saint-Jean-Cap-Ferrat** is a delight and has a small marina with sweeping vistas towards distant Monaco.

Guarding the southern tip of the cape is **le Phare**, a lighthouse which used to be open to the public but is now on one of the many **walking trails** which are a memorable way to discover Cap Ferrat. Wander through its pine forests, along its shores and by the half-hidden

Opposite: *Once a free port for the transportation of salt, the beautiful and sheltered village of Villefranche has been used as a naval base in more recent years.*
Right: *Adorning Saint-Jean-Cap-Ferrat is the elegant Villa Ephrussi de Rothschild, now open as a museum.*

villas. For those with kids, the **Parc Zoologique** (open daily) makes an interesting detour. Cap Ferrat's small-ish, pebble beaches are also pleasant: northeast-facing **Plage Paloma** and west-facing **Plage de Passable** are the favourites.

Villefranche-sur-Mer **

There are two Villefranches: new Villefranche-sur-Mer (not on the sea), a modern town that clings to the mountainside overlooking the bay, and below, on the water's edge, old Villefranche-sur-Mer, a tiny medieval town founded in 1295 by Charles II of Anjou, protected by a star-shaped **citadel** now housing the **Hôtel de Ville**, an open-air theatre, gardens, and an assortment of **free museums**.

In the 16th century, Villefranche was an important port for the exportation of salt. Medieval Villefranche, just behind place du Conseil, is small, dark and riddled with narrow streets. Its **rue Obscure** is an extraordinary vaulted medieval alley under old buildings, which leads almost from one side of old Villefranche to the other. The **Chapelle Saint-Pierre**, a 14th-century Romanesque building, was decorated by Jean Cocteau and is dedicated to the local fishermen.

Beaulieu-sur-Mer **

A fashionable address for wintering on the Riviera, well-manicured Beaulieu has a popular casino, the beautifully ornate *belle époque* **la Rotonde** (used for conferences), and **Villa Kerylos** (open daily from 10:30; 15 December to 14 February afternoons only), a replica of an ancient Greek residence. It was built between 1902 and 1908 by Théodore Reinach as a replica of a 2nd-century-BC villa on the island of Delos. Replicas of some of Antiquities greatest sculptures, some genuine Greek works, mosaics and frescoes can also be enjoyed in this unusual museum.

ÈZE, A PERFECT VILLAGE PERCHÉ

Èze, one of the **Riviera's gems**, dates back to the Bronze Age. As the crow flies, it is just behind Monaco but the road winds some 7km (nearly 5 miles) up the mountainside and onto the Moyenne Corniche. The village is almost picture post-card perfect: narrow cobbled alleys, pots of vivid flowers, carefully hidden electricity wires, and no needless publicity. Don't miss **La Poterne**, the double fortified gateway you pass through to enter the village; or the **Maison des Riquiers**, the 15th-century residence of the Lords of Èze. Wander into the **Jardin Exotique** from which, amid cacti, the views towards Corsica, are superb. On leaving the village, two of France's most famous *parfumeries* merit a stop: **Galimard** has a museum and sales outlet, while **Fragonard** has a factory and a shop.

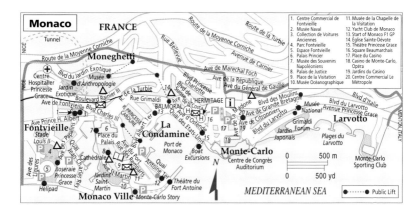

1. Centre Commercial de Fontvieille
2. Musée Naval
3. Collection de Voitures Anciennes
4. Parc Fontvieille
5. Espace Fontvieille
6. Palais Princier
7. Musée des Souvenirs Napoléoniens
8. Palais de Justice
9. Place de la Visitation
10. Musée Océanographique
11. Musée de la Chapelle de la Visitation
12. Yacht Club de Monaco
13. Start of Monaco F1 GP
14. Église Sainte-Dévote
15. Théâtre Princesse Grace
16. Square Beaumarchais
17. Place du Casino
18. Casino de Monte-Carlo, Opéra
19. Jardins du Casino
20. Centre Commercial Le Metropole

MONACO

At just short of 2km² (0.77 sq miles) Monaco is one of the smallest states in the world, but what it lacks in size it makes up for in style. Monaco is the Hong Kong of Europe: a small independent state surrounded by a foreign country, a haven for the wealthy seeking relief from taxes, and an almost crime-free playground for the rich and famous. Some 30,000 people live in the principality, 80 per cent of them foreign.

The state comprises the original settlement of Monaco, extending out like a thumb on rocky headland into the Mediterranean, and the area of Monte-Carlo known for its casino. Short of territory, Monaco's current ruler, Prince Rainier III, has reclaimed land from the sea and invested the principality with tourism and non-polluting industries.

Monaco Ville

This is the area located on the **Rock**, the historic area of Monaco. The Grimaldis live in the **Palais Princier** on **place du Palais**, originally founded by the Genoese in 1215. Tourists come to watch the Changing of the Guard at precisely 11:55 and they may also visit the sumptuous **Grands Appartements** (open daily June to October). Within the palace walls is the **Musée des Souvenirs Napoléoniens** with its collection of First-Empire memorabilia and the principality's archives.

THE GRIMALDI DYNASTY

On 8 January 1297, disguised as a monk, Guelf sympathizer François Grimaldi took the Ghibelline fortress on the Rock at Monaco. Just 49 years later, Charles I Grimaldi began erecting a solid base from which he was to rule over the neighbouring areas of Roquebrune and Menton. Thus began 700 years of rule in which the Grimaldis had an ever-changing relationship with their neighbours. In 1861, Prince Charles III Grimaldi gave up his rights to Roquebrune and Menton, which were ceded to France, and Monaco accepted its independence. The current ruler, Prince Rainier III, was born in 1923. He married American Grace Kelly in 1956, but Princess Grace died in a tragic road accident in 1982, leaving behind her husband and three children – Caroline, Albert and Stephanie.

Musée Océanographique ★★★

One of Monaco's highlights, the Oceanographic Museum was set up by Prince Albert I as part of the Institute of the same name. The imposing Italianate building, rising steeply above the sea, houses a fabulous **aquarium** where marine flora and fauna from a wide range of different environments thrive in 90 different tanks. Some of the floors are devoted to laboratories, and there is a cinema projecting fascinating films about the marine world. Also, don't miss all the skeletal exhibits.

La Vieille Ville ★★★

In this, the heart of old Monaco, houses cling to each other in tiny, sometimes vaulted streets. Of particular interest here is the **Palais de Justice**, evoking the architecture of neighbouring Italy, the **Chapelle de la Paix**, and the **Jardins Saint-Martin**, where poet Guillaume Appollinaire found inspiration.

The 1875 **Cathédrale**, fashioned from white La Turbie stone, was constructed to replace the former 12th-century church dedicated to Saint Nicholas. It has, among its artistic treasures, an altarpiece by Niçois **Louis Bréa**.

Modern Monaco ★★

Moving away from the old, the highway sweeps around **La Condamine**, its spectacular yacht harbour and watersports centre, and on to Monte-Carlo. Hidden behind the busy freeway is the 11th-century **Église Sainte-Dévote**, which houses the ruling family's votive chapel.

Le Jardin Exotique has a fine collection of some 6000 varieties of semi-desert flora. For the cactus lover, it is a real treat.

GREEK ORIGINS FOR MONACO

Although primitive Ligurian tribes inhabited Monaco around the 6th century BC, it is believed that the name 'Monaco' derives from the days of the Greeks who founded a settlement here as long ago as the 4th century BC. Monaco was associated at this time with the cult of Herakles, and it is thought that the word 'Monaco' derived from the expression *Herakles Monoïkis*, or 'Herkles Alone'. More weight is given to this argument as the port in Monaco has always been known as the Port de Hercules.

Below: *Home to Monaco's royal family, the Palais Princier dominates the place du Palais.*

MONTE-CARLO

For many the only reason for coming to Monte-Carlo is pleasure: shopping, dining and the **Casino**. This elegant building is one of the two works designed for Monaco by Charles Garnier. It was built in 1878.

The second Garnier work is the **Opera House**, a fine building where performances of world-class standard are staged annually during the November–March season. It is on a par with the grandiose Opera House in Paris, another building by the same architect.

Le Jardin Japonais *

A fine garden in the best of Zen traditions, the peaceful Japanese Garden occupies an area of over 7000m^2 (nearly two acres) – a perfect spot to relax and unwind. Among its attractions is the Japanese tea ceremony.

Beausoleil *

At the highest level of the principality lies the town of Beausoleil, technically part of the French province Alpes Maritimes. A pleasant place where even the pavements have a sunny face engraved in them, it developed at the beginning of the 20th century and, like the **Cap-d'Ail** on the shore, has a suitably elegant *belle époque* feel to it.

La Turbie *

La Turbie is noted mainly for the remains of its Roman monument, *La Trophée des Alpes*, a glorious edifice erected to commemorate Augustus' successful 15–14BC campaigns to subjugate 44 Alpine tribes. It was dedicated in 6–5BC and although a handful of Doric columns and part of its pedestal are all that remain, it is still worth visiting if only for the magnificent views of the Côte d'Azur.

Gorbio *

A pleasant little village where time has stood still, Gorbio makes an interesting excursion away from the coast through olive groves, and fruit orchards, into the cooler interior. The large elm tree in the main square dates from 1713.

Roquebrune-Cap-Martin *

Roquebrune-Cap-Martin is a fashionable place to live (or have a holiday villa). Eager historians will be delighted by the pudding-stone château that crowns this beautiful medieval town. This impressive fortress (with even more impressive views) dates from the 10th century but was later remodelled by the Grimaldis. The small town is geared for tourism and offers some good restaurants and interesting art galleries.

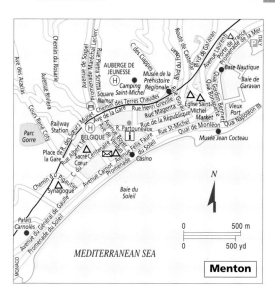

Menton **

Menton manages to combine the pleasures of a beach resort (its beaches are wide and long) with the interest of a medieval centre. It has added to this a rather unattractive modern town and a busy casino, thus capitalizing on all types of tourism. It is just a couple of kilometres from the Italian border and the influence of Italy, already strong along this coast, is particularly noticeable here.

Menton is noted for its microclimate which favours the cultivation of citrus fruits and bananas. The annual **Lemon Festival** in February celebrates the lemon with hundreds of impressive lemon 'sculptures'. The town's gardens are also a major feature and visitors should take time to explore at least the **Jardin Botanique Exotique** and the **Jardin des Colombières**.

Opposite *The annual Lemon Festival in Menton sees some innovative and impressive sculptures created from lemons.*

MUSÉE DE LA CASTRE

In the midst of Cannes' Le Suquet (see page 96), this 12th-century château and chapel, formerly occupied by the monks of Lérins, is now a museum (open morning and afternoon, except Tuesday). It offers a number of interesting **archaeological exhibits** from all parts of the Mediterranean and an important collection of **musical instruments** representing musical traditions from many different parts of the globe.

It is quite a steep climb to **Église Saint-Michel**, a church with some nice though fairly unremarkable paintings, but you get a feel for the old town on the way. Down on the shore, the **Musée Jean Cocteau** is housed in a converted 17th-century fort, **Le Bastion**. It houses a collection of the artist's ceramics, poetry, pottery and paintings. One of his breathtaking murals can be seen in the **Salle des Mariages**.

Above: *The Jean Cocteau Museum in Menton is housed in a fort.*
Opposite: *Saorge is said to be the most beautiful village in the country.*

BEYOND THE COAST

In the hilly and forested Alpes Maritimes due north of Monaco, also easily accessible from Nice, are a number of interesting villages and a series of gorges that make a fine alternative excursion to a trip along the Riviera.

Peillon, a picturesque perched village, dates back to the Middle Ages. Much of its attraction is due to the period homes and cobbled streets and when the chatter of tourists subsides you could feel as though you were in a different era. Look at the moving wall paintings by Jean Canavesio in Peillon's **Chapelle des Pénitents Blancs**.

Just 43km (27 miles) from Nice and half that distance from Menton, Sospel and Lucéram are almost on the border with Italy (indeed they have a certain Italianate atmosphere). Both are picturesque towns reached by a meandering and beautiful route that offers superb views.

Sospel celebrates 3000 years of history and is proud of its **Pont-Vieux** dating back to the 13th century, the elegant Baroque **place Saint-Michel** dominated by the 17th-century **Cathédrale Saint-Michel**, and the 19th-century **Fort du Barbonnet** just out of the village. Sospel also houses four of the carriages from the legendary **Orient Express** train.

Lucéram, known for its olive oil, is noted in particular for its religious paintings by Ludovic Bréa, one of the most talented artists active in Nice, Monaco and Liguria in the 15th century. In the church of Sainte-Marguerite there is a fine retable attributed to him.

THE PENITENTS

The Penitents, a series of laic associations, were formed in the 13th century. They comprise the White Penitents of the Holy Cross, the Black Penitents of the Misericordia, the Blue Penitents of the Holy Sepulchre and the Red Penitents of the Holy Trinity. They rose to prominence in the Baroque era when they assumed a role of social assistance for society's outcasts: orphans, the sick and dying. These associations, identified by their long robes and shrouded heads, often participate in the big religious festivals throughout France.

Saorge is classified as one of the most beautiful villages in France. Due to its narrow alleys and old stone buildings it has been likened to a Tibetan village. There is a fine Baroque church with cloisters where the *Life of Saint Francis* is depicted in an 18th-century fresco cycle.

Highlight of the small village of **Tende** is its 16th-century **Notre-Dame de l'Assumption**, though Jean Canavasio's 15th-century frescoes in the church of **Notre-Dame-des-Fontaines**, to the southeast of Tende, are probably even more interesting. From Tende it is a short trip to the **Vallée des Merveilles** (*see* panel) in the Parc National du Mercantour.

The **Vallée de la Vésubie** is an impressive gorge – the best views are from the panoramic lookout at Madone d'Utelle just above the village of **Utelle.** The road on either side of the gorge also affords fine vistas. The source of the Vésubie is up in the Alpine landscapes north of Saint-Martin-Vésubie and as it flows south it gathers force and slashes its way through the gorge south of Saint-Jean-la-Riviere. This valley formed part of the so-called *Route du Sel* (*see* panel, page 108) between the coast and Turin.

VALLÉE DES MERVEILLES

It is here, around Mont Bégo, that some 100,000 primitive drawings have been discovered – rock engravings that have been dated to 1800bc and are attributed to a Bronze-Age group of Ligurian shepherds who worshipped the gods Earth and Bull and the goddess Earth. This magnificent prehistoric site is closed to the general public but can be visited on a 10-km (6-mile) hike though superb mountain scenery in the company of an accredited guide. Information at Tende, tel: 04 93 04 73 71.

Vallée and Gorges du Loup *

A great excursion from any of the coastal towns, the Gorges de Loup are easily accessible from Cagnes or Vence and take in many small villages. **Gourdon** perches high above the rocky chasm and merits a visit for its typical southern French atmosphere. The road to Vence crosses through **Tourettes-sur-Loup**, which celebrates its **Fêtes des Violets** (a festival of violets) in early March.

Vence **

Among the notables to visit Vence were Gide, Paul Valéry, Soutine, Dufy and Matisse, who left a beautiful legacy

in the **Chapelle du Rosaire** (av Henri Matisse, open for part of the morning and afternoon on Tuesday and Thursday, and for Sunday Mass). Matisse would turn in his grave if he saw the ugly modern buildings that now deface the old centre of town.

Despite its 19th-century façade, the small **Cathédrale** dates back to the 11th century. Among its treasures is the 15th-century **tribune**, beautifully worked in oak and pear woods, by Grasse sculptor Jacotin Bellot. It was **Marc Chagall** who designed the mosaic *Moses in the Bulrushes* in the baptistry.

Saint-Paul-de-Vence ★★★

Founded by the Greeks, this superbly picturesque perched village presiding over the Loup valley dates essentially from the 12th century and is contained within medieval walls. Its principal street, the **rue Grande**, a long and at times impossibly narrow alley, bisects the length of the village.

Below: *Saint-Paul-de-Vence is a showcase for artists, and visitors can still find some fine paintings here.*

This is one medieval village not to be missed (you'll be following in the footsteps of Modigliani, Yves Montand, Jean-Paul Sartre and Simone Signoret, to mention just a few) and despite the plethora of (expensive) art galleries and fashionable boutiques, its quaintness is almost too perfect.

The simple stone **Église Collegiale** has a 12th-century choir pierced by two lovely stained-glass windows. The **Baroque chapels** are impressive, as are the **Musée de l'Histoire de Saint-Paul** and the cemetery, last resting place of Chagall, Escoffier and the Mæghts. The famous **Colombe d'Or** is a veritable gastronomic institution with a superb atmosphere. **Fondation Mæght**, a modern art museum (*see* panel, page 96), is located on the outskirts of Saint-Paul-de-Vence and has ample parking.

Cagnes-sur-Mer ★★

Cagnes-sur-Mer is noted for its ancient **Château Grimaldi**, dating back to the early 14th century – soon after the Genoese Grimaldi family, Guelf sympathizers, fled to this region of France. Part prison, part fortress, the building was converted into a palace in the 17th century.

Above: *Modern art in the Fondation Mæght, Saint-Paul-de-Vence.*

Seeking relief for his arthritic condition, Pierre-Auguste Renoir (1841–1919) migrated to the warmer south and bought a home here in 1906. When the ageing artist did lose dexterity in his hands, he spent his remaining years painting with a brush between his teeth or strapped to his wrists. His house – left much as he knew it – has become the **Musée Renoir.** Here, ten of his canvases are on display, as are works by contemporary friends.

CANNES

Cannes has made a name for itself with glittering social and cultural events and is best known for its annual **Festival International du Film**.

It was the Romans who first discovered the Baie de Cannes, but Napoleon, too, is reputed to have admired the site on his return from Elba in 1815. It was the English aristocrat and Lord Chancellor **Lord Brougham**, however, who 'discovered' Cannes in 1834 when he was warmly welcomed at its only hotel, the Auberge Pinchinat – seduced, so it is said, by *bouillabaisse*. He built a villa here and was instrumental in bringing wealthy Britons to these sunny shores.

Today, Cannes is a major tourist destination – not so much for its sights as for its congresses, cultural events, and the celebrities one might see strolling along the

---

CHAPELLE DU ROSAIRE

This sublime chapel was designed entirely by **Matisse** (three years before his death) for the Dominican nuns who had nursed him through ill health. It is a pure delight. White and airy, it is relieved by a ceramic tile wall with schematic designs depicting the Stations of the Cross and the most glorious **stained-glass windows** in blue, yellow and turquoise which, in the morning light, daub the floor and walls with their hues. Matisse designed every aspect of this chapel, including the candlesticks, vestments and the Arab-influenced door to the confessional.

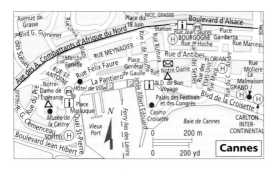

Cannes

luxurious Croisette. For an overview of the city, drive to the wooded **Croix des Gardes** or visit the **Observatoire** in Super Cannes.

Vieille Ville **

The heart of old Cannes focuses on the **Vieux Port**, a small harbour (most of the smarter yachts are moored in the Port Pierre Canto on the other side of the Baie de Cannes) just to the west of glitzy **la Croisette** where you can catch a boat to the offshore islands. It abuts the small hill known as **Le Suquet**, which offers fantastic views of Cannes and was the site of the original Roman settlement.

The small alleyways, many dating from the 19th century, evoke historic Cannes, as does the statue of Lord Brougham. The Gothic-style church, **Notre-Dame-de-l'Esperance**, dates from 1632 and marks the centre of town. Take a stroll down the pedestrian-only **rue Meynadier** where local artisans exhibit their goods, through the daily morning **Marché Forville**, a fine Provençal market much frequented by locals. There is also the colourful flower market and, on Mondays, a flea market. If that doesn't appeal, visit the city's smartest boutiques along **rue d'Antibes**.

La Croisette **

Known as the **Avenue of the Stars**, this beautiful boulevard graced by palms runs from the Palais round the bay to the Pointe Croisette where the casino is located. At its western end the much photographed (though not particularly aesthetic) **Palais des Festivals et des Congrès** hosts the annual **Festival International du Film**. Since its inception in 1946 it has become Europe's premier cinematic event. The many handprints of film stars past and present decorate the pavement in the nearby **Allée des Stars**.

FONDATION MÆGHT

Founded by Marguerite and Aimé Mæght, art dealers from Cannes, this is an unique experience in modern art. Housed in an innovative building designed by Catalan **Jose Luis Sert**, it presents works by some of the 20th-century greats. You enter through the gates and gardens, where sculptures by, among many others, **Miró**, **Giacometti** and **Calder** decorate the space, cross over a couple of pools and fine yourself among the paintings and sculpture that define the development of art in the 20th century. Ceramics, mosaics, glasswork and fountains complement the collection of paintings and drawings. Look out for works by **Bonnard**, **Chagall**, **Léger**, Giacometti and Miró, and don't miss the small chapel with its 13th-century wooden sculpture and simple purple-and-white stained-glass windows by **Georges Braque**.

The Croisette is where Cannes' smartest hotels are to be found, the 1911 **Carlton Hotel** being the city's landmark to luxury. Don't miss **La Malmaison**, a fine 1863 building originally part of the Grand Hotel. It hosts temporary exhibitions of modern art.

For those wishing to try their hand at gambling, Cannes offers the **Casino Croisette** in the Palais des Festivals, the **Carlton Casino Club** and the smart **Palm Beach Casino** on Pointe Croisette.

ANTIBES-JUAN-LES-PINS

One of the most gracious and attractive towns along the Côte d'Azur, Antibes straddles the peninsular Cap d'Antibes which extends like a horse's head into the Golfe-Juan (where **Napoleon** returned from banishment in Elba). The cape itself is the domain of ultra luxury, crowned at **Eden-Roc** by a stately hotel and restaurant of the same name. Pine trees hide exclusive homes and the indented shoreline makes a perfect spot for canoeing or a dip. Beaches on the northern side of the peninsula are pleasant and sandy, while those on the south, technically in Juan-les-Pins, are cluttered with rows of clubs and their quota of beach beds. Antibes and Juan-les-Pins merge and it is difficult to know where one ends and the other starts. Generally speaking, Antibes is the older part and includes the area along the cape, while Juan-les-Pins is its more modern seaside sibling.

The sheltered bays found along the coast around Antibes were known to the Greeks who soon founded the city of Antipolos, which was later to form part of a Roman province, Alpae Maritimae. By around 1850 the area began to welcome wealthy tourists among whom, in the 1920s, were plenty of Americans (Scott Fitzgerald among others) who brought with them jazz – hence its present fame as a prime venue for jazz festivals (*see* page 99).

> ### ILES DE LÉRINS
>
> One of the most popular excursions from the Côte d'Azur resorts, is to take a 15-minute boat ride to the two Iles de Lérins.
> **Ile Sainte-Marguerite**, 3km (nearly 2 miles) in length, is covered with thick vegetation and is a popular place with ramblers. It boasts the **Fort Royal**, reconstructed by Vauban in 1712, which today houses archaeological marine exhibits in its **Musée de la Mer**. In the late 17th century the fort numbered among its prisoners the mysterious man in an iron mask.
> **Ile Saint-Honorat** is the smaller of the two islands and is still owned by the Cistercian monks of Sénanque. Some 25 men divide their time between prayer and work, cultivating lavender, rosemary, vines and making a liqueur called lérina from a mixture of 44 plants and white grapes. Their Abbey de Lérins may be visited.

Below: *The imposing façade of the Carlton Hotel characterizes Cannes' La Croisette beach.*

A TRIP IN THE *VISIOBULLE*

Antibes from a different perspective? The *Visiobulle* motors out from Juan-les-Pins seven times daily in summer. It cruises around the millionaire's district of Cap d'Antibes, affording splendid views of the cape and its homes. Its main attraction, however, is the submarine viewing of flora and fauna through the glass-bottom hull. For information, tel: 04 93 67 02 11.

Below: *The old town of Antibes has retained its timeless charm.*

Antibes Town ★★

The most appealing parts of town beyond the **remparts de Vauban** are the **Port Vauban** and **Vieille Ville**. The narrow streets are delightful and exploited to the maximum by small shops, restaurants and proud homeowners. Impeccably clean and bowing under beautiful window boxes and flowering plants, they are a pleasure to roam. The **Marché Provençal** near **place Nationale** is a good place to pick up local herbs, fruit and vegetables, soaps and olive oils.

Opposite the handsome **cathedral** (built between the 12th and 17th centuries on the site of a Roman temple) is the **Château Grimaldi**, which houses the **Musée Picasso**. To be seen here are some priceless drawings, ceramics and canvases by Pablo Picasso, some of them executed during his 1946 stay in the château. Of particular interest are the many ceramic dishes and vases which he produced in Vallauris when he began to experiment with clay as a medium. There are also some works by **Hans Hartung**, another artist who made Antibes his home, and outside there are a number of sculptures by other 20th-century artists.

Housed in the **Bastion Saint-André** (Fort Saint André, built by military architect Vauban) is the interesting **Musée d'Histoire et d'Archéologie**. The route around Cap d'Antibes was a prime shipping route for the Romans, but due to its rocky nature shipwrecks were a common occurrence along this stretch of coast. Many of the amphorae, coins and jewels that once formed precious cargo are now on display here.

Juan-les-Pins ★

Antibes' more raucous sibling Juan-les-Pins has quite a different atmosphere. Its adherents lie in the sun all day and party all night. The action centres on the crossroads between *Pam-Pam* and *Crystal* just opposite the popular discotheque and continues well into the small hours.

Vallauris *

Minutes away from the coast, and situated among pines and olives, the town of Vallauris has had a reputation for its ceramics since Roman times. It became famous when Picasso spent some time here from 1948–55 to learn the art of pottery.

Above: *Beach resort* par excellence, *Juan-les-Pins.*

The **Musée Municipale** which includes the Musée Magnelli and the adjoining **Musée National Picasso** (open Wednesday to Monday, morning and afternoon) traces the history of pottery in the town from its earliest days and also embraces an excellent collection of items (donated by painter Alberto Magnelli) from the pre-Columbian days of Mexico and Guatemala. In addition it includes an excellent range of Vallauris ceramics by local masters, the Massier family, and modern greats such as Capron and Gerbino whose work is every bit as good as, if not better than, that of their more famous colleague, Picasso. Picasso's works are to be found in the peaceful, small chapel next door to the museum. Here, his 1952 works *La Guerre* and *La Paix* decorate the walls and items of pottery are displayed around the room.

Another museum worth a visit is the **Musée de la Poterie** (open daily morning and afternoon) where an old pottery has been faithfully reconstructed. All through town displays of pottery and ceramics spill out of scores of galleries and shops onto the pavements. Take time to visit one of the town's most prestigious galleries, **Sassi-Millici**, to see work of other local modern masters.

JAZZ AT JUAN-LES-PINS

It was in the 1920s that the Americans first discovered Juan-les-Pins. They brought with them a zest for life and their music of the moment, jazz. Sidney Bechet is said to have fallen in love with the place, likening it to New Orléans. His 1951 marriage was a memorable fête for the glitterati and required Dixieland performers and irrepressible dancers. In 1960 the first jazz festival took place and since then performers have numbered Count Basie, Duke Ellington, Dizzy Gillespie, Miles Davis and Ella Fitzgerald, to name but a handful. The annual jazz festival (held each July) has now become an established event.

Above: *A huge mural decorates the exterior of the Musée National Fernand Léger, at Biot.*
Opposite: *The blending of fragrances to create a perfume is a subtle art.*

Biot *

Known for its fine pottery, glassblowing and the old fortifications, the hilltop-hugging town of Biot is also renowned for its **Musée National Fernand Léger** (2km – just over a mile – out of town along the chemin du Val de Pome, open Wednesday to Monday, morning and afternoon). This magnificent museum stands on what was Léger's own property (he died here in 1955). You're welcomed by the glorious spectacle of a huge Léger decorating the wall of the museum which contains over 450 of his works (bright paintings, gouaches, drawings, glassware and colourful ceramics). The gardens, too, ought not to be missed.

For fun of a different kind, the aquatic park, **Marineland**, offers the largest marine show in Europe featuring whales, dolphins and sea lions. A museum gives you insight into the marine environment, while children will also enjoy a visit to the **Aquasplash** and the butterfly farm **La Jungle des Papillons**.

Mougins **

Just 15 minutes from Cannes, Mougins brims with the secondary homes of the wealthy. The **Vieux** village is an imposing hilltop settlement dating back to the 15th century set amid pines, olive trees and cypresses. Its old homes, many of which have been meticulously renovated, have attracted film stars and other celebrity personalities over the years, including Christian Dior, Man Ray, Catherine Deneuve, Edith Piaf, Jean Cocteau and Pablo Picasso (who died here). Mougins is also noted for its fine dining and boasts a handful of the best restaurants in the south of France, including the famous **Moulin de Mougins**.

The **Musée de l'Automobiliste** (chemin Font de Currault, open daily from mid-December to mid-November) is a must for lovers of veteran cars.

The **Musée de la Photographie** at 67 rue de l'Église will appeal to photographers. It contains photos of Picasso, a gift from photographer André Villiers. Also on show are old pictures of Mougins and an assortment of antiquated cameras.

Grasse **

For the French, the very name of this small town is synonymous with **perfume**. And indeed, after visiting one of the perfume factories here, you too will carry the fragrance with you. This small but elegant town is home to three major perfume companies, **Fragonard**, **Galimard** and **Molinard** (all open daily and offering guided tours), who between them have created many a famous perfume.

The **Musée International de la Parfumerie**, 8 place du Cours (open daily June to September; Wednesday to Saturday during October, and mid-December to May) will put the industry, and Grasse, into perspective.

The 18th-century French painter Jean-Honoré Fragonard (1732–1806) was born in Grasse. In the 17th-century villa that was once his home you will find the **Villa Musée Fragonard** (same opening hours as above), where you have the chance to see some of his works and those of his family. The Fragonard heritage is also displayed in another museum located above the **Perfumerie Fragonard** in the centre of town. This one offers an interesting collection of historic, often exotic perfume bottles and laboratory utensils.

Lastly, and definitely not to be missed, is the **Musée d'Art et d'Histoire de Provence** set in an 18th-century Provençal mansion. It reproduces the atmosphere of historic Provence through ceramics, paintings, costume and furniture, and also has a typical French garden.

THE ART OF GLASSWARE

The ancient art of glass making has become a Provençal tradition since it was brought to the country in the 16th century. The art flourished especially in the forested areas of Provence where wood was in abundant supply. Sadly, the industry has declined since the advent of machine-made glass and only a few master glass-blowers continue the art. Lovers of glass objects should visit Jean-Claude Novaro's gallery, **Le Patrimoine**, in Biot, where the master produces extremely beautiful works. Le Patrimoine, 2 place aux Arcades, Biot, tel: 04 93 65 60 23.

Côte d'Azur and Alpes Maritimes at a Glance

BEST TIMES TO VISIT

The Côte d'Azur has plenty going on all year. In February and March are **festivals** such as those at Menton (Festival du Citron) and Nice (Carnival). **Winters** can be cool, though often sunny. The snow-covered mountains attract skiers. **Summers** are usually crowded, **spring** and **autumn** pleasant.

GETTING THERE

Aéroport International de Nice-Côte d'Azur (tel: 04 93 21 30 30) serves most European capitals, as well as domestic ones. Nice is linked to Paris (930km or 580 miles) by the toll-paying A8 and A7 motorways, which heads north via Lyon. Marseille is 190km (119 miles) west. *Autoroutes*, *routes nationales* and well-maintained *routes départementales* link all the towns in the area. **Buses** connect Nice with Paris, Marseille and Italy. Information from the *Gare Routière*, the bus station, tel: 04 93 85 61 81. Nice is a major stop on the **railway** and fast intercity connections. The TGV (not yet all high-speed) service connects the city with Lyon and Paris, while Grandes Lignes connect Nice with Montpellier and Spain, and eastwards Italy. For all railway information tel: 08 36 35 35 35, or for English-language operators 08 36 35 35 39. For sea crossings to and from Corsica (including day tours), contact SNCM Ferry-terranée on tel: 04 93 13 66 69.

GETTING AROUND

It is simplest to hire a car (on arrival at the airport), but there are also good bus and train links along the coast. The **Cars Phocéens** (tel: 04 93 39 94 52) run sightseeing trips, local transport services and long-distance buses. Otherwise contact the *Gare Routière*, the bus station, tel: 04 93 85 61 81 for details of services. The **Sunbus** service offers multi-day tickets for sightseeing around Nice, tel: 04 93 16 52 10 for details. The **SNCF** has frequent **rail services** between coastal towns from Fréjus to Menton and the Italian border. In peak season it is easier to take the train than to endure the congested coastal routes. Many towns offer *Petit Train* itineraries along the roads to the major sights. A bit of an eyesore, they do give a sense of orientation, and take in many sights in a short time.

WHERE TO STAY

LUXURY

L'Hermitage, square Beaumarchais, Monte-Carlo, tel: (00 377) 04 92 16 40 00, fax: 92 16 38 52, e-mail: resort@sbm.mc One of Europe's most exclusive addresses. Eiffel designed the dome in the winter garden. **Hôtel Négresco**, 37 promenade des Anglais, Nice, tel: l04 93 16 64 00, fax: 93 88 35 68, e-mail: reservations@hotel-negresco.com Nice's famous seafront hotel, ultra chic and well-placed.

Carlton Inter-Continental, 58 bd Croisette, Cannes, tel: 04 93 06 40 06, fax: 93 06 40 25, e-mail: cannes@interconti.com The grandest address in Cannes, right on the Croisette. **Voile d'Or**, au port, St-Jean-Cap-Ferrat, tel: 04 93 01 13 13, fax: 93 76 11 17. Fine hotel overlooking the port towards Monaco. Good restaurant. **Hôtel du Cap Eden Roc**, bd Kennedy, Antibes, tel: 04 93 61 39 01, fax: 93 67 76 04, e-mail: edenroc-hotel@ wanadoo.fr Exclusive address with private beach. Renowned restaurant.

MID-RANGE

Hôtel Balmoral, 12 av de la Costa, Monte-Carlo, tel: (00 377) 93 50 623, fax: 93 15 086. An old hotel in a good location just above the marina. **Brise Marine**, av Mermoz, Saint-Jean-Cap-Ferrat, tel: 04 93 76 04 36, fax: 93 76 11 49. Family-run hotel with superb location and pleasant gardens. **Villa Roseraie**, av H Giraud, 06140 Vence, tel: 04 93 58 02 20, fax: 93 58 99 31, e-mail: rvilla5536@aol.fr Charming small Provençal hotel, with each room individually styled. **Hôtel Ste-Valerie**, rue de l'Orotoire, Juan-les-Pins, tel: 04 93 61 07 15, fax: 93 61 47 52, e-mail: saintevalerie@juanlespins.net A mid-sized hotel with pool, quiet street. Private beach.

Côte d'Azur and Alpes Maritimes at a Glance

BUDGET

Hôtel Suisse, 15 quai Raubà-Capéù, Nice, tel: 04 92 17 39 00, fax: 93 85 30 70. Great position overlooking the Promenade des Anglais.

Hôtel St-Góthard, 20 rue Paganini, Nice, tel: 04 93 88 13 41, fax: 93 82 27 55. Near station and pr des Anglais.

Hôtel Boeri, 29 bd Gén Leclerc, Beausoleil, tel: 04 93 78 38 10, fax: 04 93 41 90 95. Ideal for visiting Monte-Carlo (two minutes by foot).

Hôtel Florian, 8 rue Cmdt André, Cannes, tel: 04 93 39 24 82, fax: 04 92 99 18 30. Small modernized hotel, two minutes' walk from beach and 5 minutes from the port.

WHERE TO EAT

LUXURY

Chantecler, Hôtel Négresco (see Where to Stay). Innovative cuisine in traditional setting.

Louis XV, Hôtel de Paris, place Casino, Monte-Carlo, tel: (00 377) 92 16 30 01. One of Monaco's highest-rated restaurants.

Colombe d'Or, St-Paul-de-Vence, tel: 04 93 32 80 02. Famous terrace and restaurant at entry to old town. Renowned cuisine. Some rooms.

Belle Otéro, Hôtel Carlton, (see Where to Stay). Fine cuisine.

Le Moulin de Mougins, 424 chemin du Moulin Quartier Nôtre Dame de Vie, Mougins, tel: 04 93 75 78 24. In an old olive oil mill, more traditional than innovative.

Belles Rives, 33 bd Beaudoin, Antibes, tel: 04 93 61 02 79. One of the best for fine cuisine.

MID-RANGE

La Petite Maison, 11 rue St-François de Paul, Vieux Nice, tel: 04 93 92 59 59. Fresh, innovative Mediterranean cuisine.

Le Café de Turin, place Garibaldi, Nice, tel: 04 93 62 29 52. A renowned oyster bar in the heart of town.

Café de Paris, place Casino, Monte-Carlo, tel: (00 377) 92 16 20 20. Brasserie atmosphere, variety of menus and prices.

Mesclun, 16 rue St-Antoine, Cannes, tel: 04 93 99 45 19. Dinner only. Very popular restaurant in old part of town.

Couleur Pourpre, 7 rempart Ouest, St-Paul-de-Vence, tel: 04 93 32 60 14. Cosy, good views, excellent cuisine. Reservations recommended.

BUDGET

Lou Pistou, 4 rue Terrasse, Nice, tel: 04 93 62 21 82. Noted for its cuisine niçoise.

La Farigoule, 78 bd Carnot, Cannes, tel: 04 93 39 22 23. Authentic Provençal cuisine at fairly affordable prices.

TOURS AND EXCURSIONS

ATE Excursions (in train) along the coast and inland to Haute-Provence. For information in Cannes, tel: 04 93 24 81 25, or consult the website: www.ate-excursions.com The *French Riviera* motor cruiser offers lunch and dinner cruises off the Riviera, departing from Cannes. Not inexpensive, but very memorable. For details tel: 04 93 68 98 98.

USEFUL CONTACTS

Office de tourisme, 11 pl Gén de Gaulle, Antibes, tel: 04 92 90 53 00.

Office de tourisme, Palais des Festivals, espl du Prés Georges Pompidou, Cannes, tel: 04 93 39 24 53.

Office de tourisme, 22 cours H Crespi, Grasse, tel: 04 93 36 66 66.

Office de tourisme, 2A bd des Moulins, Monte-Carlo, tel: (00 377) 93 41 09 11.

Office de tourisme, 5 prom des Anglais, Nice, tel: 04 92 14 48 00.

Aéroport International de Nice-Côte d'Azur, tel: 04 93 21 30 30.

NICE	J	F	M	A	M	J	J	A	S	O	N	D
AVERAGE TEMP. °F	48	49	52	55	62	68	74	74	70	62	54	50
AVERAGE TEMP. °C	8	9	11	12	16	20	23	23	21	16	12	10
HOURS OF SUN DAILY	4	6	7	8	10	11	12	11	9	7	6	5
RAINFALL in	2.8	2.8	2.8	2.4	1.6	1.2	0.4	1.2	2.4	4.3	4.3	3.1
RAINFALL mm	70	70	70	60	40	30	10	30	60	110	110	80
DAYS OF RAINFALL	1	1	2	2	3	3	3	4	3	5	2	1

6
Le Var

Although its name may not immediately strike a chord, the Var is very definitely maritime Provence at its best. Beyond the upland areas often cloaked in dense forests of pine or oak and the small secluded valleys favouring vineyards, there are sandy beaches, small coves and rocky headlands, yachts and cruisers, and compact old towns that have now been revamped for the lucrative tourist trade.

The largest town on the coast is **Toulon**, tucked into a huge bay giving shelter to its important naval port. On terra firma, sailors mix with the town's many African immigrants giving it a heady cosmopolitan atmosphere.

Like many of the small ports along the Var coast, **Sanary** and **Bandol** blossom during the busy summer months, as does their more famous neighbour, **Saint-Tropez**. **Sainte-Maxime** and **Saint-Raphaël** also fill with visitors attracted to the beaches and seaside promenades. But even during the heat of summer it is possible to find some tranquillity in the hills and highlands of the magnificent **Massif de l'Esterel** and **Massif des Maures** just behind the coast. Central Var, around **Le Thoronet** and **Saint-Maximin-la-Sainte-Baume** presents yet another aspect of this region: a fine religious heritage which more than merits a detour.

Off the coast and south of the elegant town of **Hyères** – once renowned for its salt production – lies the trio of islands, the **Iles d'Hyères**, among France's most popular offshore islands. Small but interesting, Port-Cros forms one of the country's most important **national parks**.

Don't Miss

*** **Fréjus:** a fascinating Roman past.
*** **Iles d'Hyères:** a trip to these offshore islands.
** **Saint-Tropez:** see the rich and famous.
** **Le Thoronet:** a magnificent Cistercian abbey.
** **Ramatuelle and Gassin:** two small medieval villages.
** **Port Grimaud:** a modern port with a traditional feel.
* **Le Lavandou and Sainte-Maxime:** for their lovely beaches.

Opposite: *These ancient columns stand proud in Fréjus, attesting to the town's Roman past.*

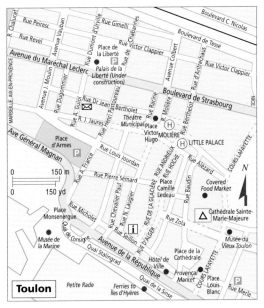

Toulon

TOULON

Bathed in the clear light of the Mediterranean, under the protective shadow of Mont Faron and sheltering in Europe's largest natural harbour, Toulon has enjoyed an excellent reputation since the Romans first recognized its maritime potential. Beyond the city limits, suburbs like La Morillon have good beaches that offer safe swimming. Though Toulon has an excellent harbour, it is better known as a naval rather than a commercial port. Like Marseille, many of its inhabitants are of non-European origins and you'll come across entire areas where Arab is the *lingua franca* or where French bistros are replaced by Chinese, Vietnamese and Tunisian restaurants. This eclectic element, combined with a strong naval force, gives Toulon an appealing and unique atmosphere.

La Vieille Ville **

The narrow, shabby streets of the old quarter are undergoing something of a renaissance at present. Many are pedestrianized, the public areas are better maintained and commerce is returning to the area, but exotic qualities still remain, for the large daily (except Monday) **Provençal market** which lines **Cours Lafayette** is still treated much like a souk by the many Moroccan, Algerian, Tunisian and Chinese residents who come searching for tropical produce and pungent spices. Halfway up the Cours Lafayette lies the former bishop's palace, **Musée du Vieux Toulon** (open Monday to

---

AOC BANDOL

A pretty port, Bandol is better known to the French for its wine, made here since the time of the Greeks. The deep red wine, largely the product of the aromatic Mourvèdre grape, is aged for a minimum of 18 months in oak casks. It is the most prestigious wine from the south coast and its area of production runs just some 16 km(10 miles) beyond Toulon. Today Bandol also produces white and rosé wines.

Saturday, morning and afternoon). This is a library and historic museum which puts much accent on the young Napoleon. The **Cathédrale Sainte-Marie-Majeure**, an unusually square building with beautiful if modern stained-glass windows, dates back to the 11th century. Through the many *rues de pietons*, you'll find your way to the **place Victor Hugo**, which is dominated by the neo-classical façade of the city's **Opera House**.

Museums *

On the harbour front are the Baroque gates that lead to the **Musée de la Marine** (place Monsenergue, open daily, morning and afternoon), which explores Toulon's naval history and exhibits a number of scale models and paintings. Other naval exhibits include the *La Dives* (at pointe de la Mitre), a former tank carrier now converted into a floating museum in which you can get an idea of life on board a military vessel. In the **Tour Royale**, next door, is the **Musée Naval de la Tour Royale**. The fort was built by Louis XII in 1514 and along with prisoners' graffiti on the dungeon walls you can see more naval exhibits.

Above: *The cosmopolitan atmosphere in Toulon is never more evident than in its huge daily market.*
Below: *Fort Balaguier was built by military architect Vauban in 1676 to defend the port of Toulon.*

Sanary-sur-Mer *

This small resort town was once the gathering point for German writers fleeing Nazi Germany, among them Thomas Mann, Franz Werfel and Bertold Brecht. (Many of them left France during 1942 for the safety of the United States.) Today, the charming little port is one of the more pleasant on the coast, without too many pretensions but with the right amount of cachet.

Above: Known mainly for its excellent wine, Bandol also has an attractive sailing port.

Bandol *

The port of Bandol lacks the charm of its neighbours. It is still popular, but probably better known for the wines carrying the **Bandol** label. The Romans were instrumental in starting the industry which is still going strong. One of the main attractions at Bandol is the **Jardin Exotique et Zoo de Sanary-Bandol** (open daily except Sunday morning), which has a fine collection of tropical plants.

HYÈRES

This pleasant town has long been one of the most popular winter resorts in the south of France and with good reason. The climate is clement, the town has a fascinating history and its panorama is impressive.

Hyères looks out over a verdant and fertile landscape towards the **Presqu'île de Giens**, a nub of wooded land crowned by the little village of Giens which, if the sea rose just a couple of metres, would constitute an island. At present it is not, as the oddity is joined to the mainland by saline marshes (salt has been a mainstay of the town's economy for centuries) that constitute a breeding ground for flamingos and other wetland wildlife. This no-man's land is fringed on either side by sandy beaches. Further afield lie the picturesque **Iles d'Hyères** which are administered by the town.

The heart of the old town is the old quarter which took form on the site occupied by the town of Olbia in the 4th century BC. Hyères boasts two main churches: that of **Saint-Louis** and the 12–13th-century collegiate church, **Saint-Paul**. The 13th-century **Porte Massillon** leads into the old town, and further up the hill you'll come across the medieval tower left by the **Knights Templar**. Crowning the heights are the remains of a 12–13th-century **château**.

SALTY PAST

The swampy flatlands just south of the town of Hyères have been the site of salt production for centuries. Salt was, in historic times, essential for the preservation of food and for tanning leather. At its height of production, Hyères exported salt in two ways: either through the freeport at Villefranche, which owed much of its fortune to the salt trade, or via endless mule trains along the so-called *Route du Sel*. During its heyday in the 16th and 17th centuries, Hyères loaded up over 30,000 mules each year, sending salt supplies to towns north of the Alps.

But Hyères is not all medieval. The 18th and 19th centuries were a golden time for the town and many a handsome villa and municipal building dates from this era. Look out for the lovely **Villa Tunisienne** and take time to stop by the **Grand Hôtel des Iles d'Or**.

You will also notice the plethora of palms – Hyères is one of Europe's largest producers of palms, hence the new town, **Hyères-les-Palmiers**.

Iles d'Hyères ★★★

Just off the coast from Hyères lie the three islands known as the Iles d'Hyères – **Porquerolles**, **Port-Cros** and the largely off-limits **Ile du Levant**. The first two have accommodation; the last is for the most part a military area without public access. Regular ferries between Hyères and le Lavandou service these islands (with additional services during the summer months).

The islands offer a pleasant escape from the mainland and unique flora and fauna. Port-Cros has been designated a national park and, with its rambling paths and snorkelling trails, is a fine place to explore.

Le Lavandou ★

Once just a small fishing town, le Lavandou is now geared up for tourists in a big way with boat excursions, numerous restaurants and a popular **marina**.

Below: *Headquarters for the national park, Port-Cros is a delightful island with a port and hotel accommodation.*

Above: *A choice of superb beaches around le Lavandou has contributed to making the town a popular holiday destination.*

It has a picturesque old town filled with small backstreets and hidden squares too often overlooked by tourists, but its real attraction lies in a choice of sandy beaches and its proximity to the Iles d'Hyères for which there are regular ferries.

North of the town, the coast is dented with small creeks and bays, some sandy, others rocky. There are a number of fashionably low-key resorts along the coast, none of which have suffered the overexploitation of northern neighbour, Saint-Tropez. The hinterland of verdant mountainside – Le Massif des Maures – offers a chance to escape the small villages which have, in the last three decades, cast aside their anonymity to cash in on the holiday trade.

Le Massif des Maures **

This beautiful area of pine, chestnut and oak trees is largely undeveloped. It is a fine place for ramblers and hikers and its shady dells provide many a fine picnic spot. Rising, often steeply, to 779m (2556ft) at **La Sauvette**, it extends from the town of Hyères right up to Fréjus and Saint-Raphaël, and its width averages some 22km (14 miles) from its northwestern flanks across to the Mediterranean shore on the southeastern side. This area is known for its cork oaks from which bottle corks are produced locally, and for fine sweet chestnuts. The village of **la Garde-Freinet** celebrates the harvest with a special annual festival.

Le Corniche des Maures ***

The spectacular drive along the **Corniche des Maures** takes you past wild and rugged scenery, from Hyères through a number of popular beach resorts including

---

LAVANDOU'S DOZEN

Le Lavandou prides itself on the choice of beaches in its district. Twelve sandy expanses line the shore, either widely spaced between headlands, or hidden within small inlets. From the **Plage de l'Anglade** in the west through to the **Plage de Pramousquier** in the east, these are well-maintained, under the watchful eye of lifeguards, and easily accessible. For those without a car, the *Petit Train* runs between the beaches, taking about 50 minutes from west to east.

le **Lavandou**, **Saint-Tropez** and **Sainte-Maxime** before finishing just south of Fréjus. To do the coast justice (and due to all the bends and beach traffic), you should allow at least four hours to drive the 110km (68 miles).

The small town of **Ramatuelle** is one of the Massif's hidden treasures. The medieval town, built in circular fashion on a hill, surveys an almost evergreen slope that drops gently down to the Anse de Pampelonne, a huge sandy bay which is shared by the Ramatuelle and Saint-Tropez communes. If Saint-Tropez is loud, Ramatuelle can only be described as discreet and for those travellers who want the opportunity of dipping into the razzle and retreating, it makes an ideal base.

Gassin *

Another medieval gem, with tasteful modern suburbs (the village won an architectural award for the integration of its modern architecture with the original old part of the settlement), **Gassin** is just 5 minutes from Ramatuelle. Its tiny crooked and narrow stone streets are particularly evocative. It has another, superb southern outlook towards the sea.

Below: *Though this stretch of coastline teems with life, it is still possible to find a haven in calm, isolated waters.*

SAINT-TROPEZ

Brought to international fame by French actress, Brigitte Bardot, this once small and peaceful port in the Gulf of Saint-Tropez is now France's most glitzy resort. It is still small and in parts outrageously pretty, but the tranquillity of the area has been shattered by the presence of the rich and famous, their acolytes and the starstruck. The quaint little

Opposite: *The town of Saint-Tropez has been carefully tended to offer visitors the atmosphere of a delightful and colourful Mediterranean port.*

fishing vessels that once plied the coast for mackerel and the occasional tuna have been nudged aside by a gleaming white ocean-going cruisers, enormous motor-powered sailing ships and magnificent luxury yachts. The village has changed; Bardot, however, still remains.

La Vieille Ville ***

The port is where Saint-Tropez's action is centred and during the latter part of the day socialites mingle with the people-watchers down on the quay. The **Café de Paris** does a fine trade as its clients nurse beers, ices or pastis, facing the continual and fascinating parade. Along the pavement street artists daub their interpretations of the port, Provence, or a passing tourist who sits nervously in the public eye.

Beyond the port area, the immaculately maintained narrow streets, washed in warm Provençal hues and embellished by colourful trailing flowers, vanish into quiet squares and ancient walls where, away from the activity, life continues quietly in the shadows. Walk through the fish market, sensibly placed under an alley, breathe in the perfumes from the vegetable and herb stalls and gaze at the wonderful display of the best quality in French *primeurs* and a variety of fruits – a bounteous cornucopia of locally grown produce. Throughout the town, the siena-coloured tower of the 19th-century Baroque church pierces above the roofs, providing a convenient beacon.

It is pleasant to stroll right around the port and along the eastern seashore towards the castle. Here you'll still find a space on the rocks, a place from which you can either go for a swim or watch the myriad fish fin through the tepid waters as spinnakers fly modern yachts across the bay.

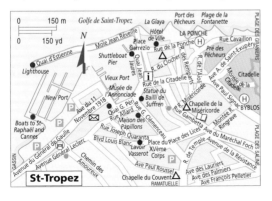

Église de Saint-Tropez *

This vividly coloured church dominates much of the village skyline. It was built in the 19th century and most people will probably find it more interesting from the outside than from within.

Musée de l'Annonciade ***

Surely one of France's most beautiful museums, the Musée (place Grammont, open morning and afternoon, daily) houses nearly 60 paintings (a gift from Georges Grammont) and a handful of sculptures by artists who lived and worked in the south of France in the late 19th and early 20th centuries. These include **Paul Signac**, **Albert Marquet** and **Henri-Edmond Cross** who produced fine paintings of Saint-Tropez. Signac discovered Saint-Tropez while sailing his yacht in the area and his canvasses, such as *Saint-Tropez, l'orage*, are particularly evocative. There are four works by **Henri Matisse**, three by that great colourist, **André Derain** and three paintings by **Edouard Vuillard**. The works are exhibited in a 16th-century ex-chapel in beautifully serene surrounds – a world away from the razzmatazz outside.

THE BEACHES

What would Saint-Tropez be without its beaches? It was here that suntanning became an art form, and adherents took off as much as possible. Today, some 30 years after the town made a name for itself, the beaches are still pulsating. The Italian penchant for rows of beach beds and parasols now threatens to consume parts of **Anse de Pampelonne** and the **Plage de Tahiti** (named for the trendy restaurant/beach club that attracts the young and nubile) though recent opposition has reversed this trend. Elsewhere, you can bare all on the sandy beach and dip your toes in the clean waters of the beautiful Baie de Pampelonne. The other attractive beach, slightly nearer to town, is on the **Baie des Canébiers**.

Grimaud *

The small town of Grimaud crowns a small hill and
looks towards the Mediterranean just 6km (3.5 miles)
away. It is a typical medieval settlement, complete
with a ruined castle, from which – thankfully – cars
are banished. The town owes its name to the Grimaldis,
this time to Gibelin de Grimaldi (AD973). The Knights
Templar connection was strong in Grimaud and one
of their houses still remains, though not open to the
public. The **rue des Templiers**, too, bears testament to
their presence here.

Port Grimaud **

Brainchild of architect François Spoerry, award-winning
Port Grimaud was constructed in the early 1960s on
90ha (222 acres) of undeveloped **marshy land** just to the
northwest of Saint-Tropez. Forty years on, Port Grimaud
is a thoroughly integrated modern marina village of
some 2500 waterside homes connected by few roads
but a maze of canals. The passage of the past decades
has comfortably weathered the Provençal architecture
into its current mellow and highly attractive form. With
many **restaurants** and upmarket **boutiques**, the Port
supports a quorum of elite residents – many of whom

moor their luxury yachts and cruisers at the bottom of their gardens – a floating colony of summer yachties and a constant influx of sightseers.

Sainte-Maxime *

This town's highlight is undoubtedly its long, lovely sandy beach on the Bay of Saint-Tropez to the south of the *vieux quartiers*. It is not yet covered by beach chairs and closed off by restaurants (though there are quite a number). Swimming is safe and good – it's an ideal place for a family holiday.

The town centres on its **port**. Behind it stretch the narrow streets of old Sainte-Maxime, covered and open markets, and stalls selling local arts and crafts. Car-free in many cases, these streets make for a pleasant stroll. The **Tour Carrée**, built in 1520 as a defensive tower against marauding pirates, now houses the **Musée des Maintenances des Traditions Locales** that is dedicated to preserving local customs. For a panoramic view of Sainte-Maxime, the Bay of Saint-Tropez, the distant Iles de Lérins and across to the Alps, drive up to the Colline du Sémaphore on a clear day.

Saint-Raphaël *

Saint-Raphaël is a large resort town on the seaboard that has slipped almost imperceptibly into Fréjus, such is the rate of expansion in each community. It is situated

THE FINEST GARDENS

In the 19th and 20th centuries, several impressive gardens were laid out in the south of France. Some are open to visitors only during the spring to autumn months, so check before visiting. Following below is a short listing encompassing a variety of styles:
Antibes: Villa Eilenroc and Parc Thuret
Beaulieu-sur-Mer: Villa Kérylos
Éze: Jardin Exotique
Mandelieu-La Napoule: Château de La Napoule
Monaco: Jardin Exotique
Nice: Gardens of the Monastère de Cimiez and the Parc Phœnix
Saint-Paul de Vence: Fondation Mæght
Saint-Jean-Cap-Ferrat: Villa Ephrussi de Rothschild
Sainte-Maxime: Jardin Botanique

Opposite: *Purpose-built around a series of canals, Port Grimaud has aged with grace into a fine port.*
Left: *Sainte-Maxime has cultivated a pleasant family-orientated ambience.*

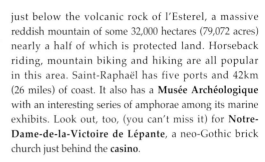

Fréjus

LE MARCHÉ NOCTURNE

During the summer months, Port de Fréjus hosts a popular evening market (daily except Wednesday and Thursday) that provides a showcase for local handicrafts and paintings. Note that it alternates from the west to the east quay, each week.

just below the volcanic rock of l'Esterel, a massive reddish mountain of some 32,000 hectares (79,072 acres) nearly a half of which is protected land. Horseback riding, mountain biking and hiking are all popular in this area. Saint-Raphaël has five ports and 42km (26 miles) of coast. It also has a **Musée Archéologique** with an interesting series of amphorae among its marine exhibits. Look out, too, (you can't miss it) for **Notre-Dame-de-la-Victoire de Lépante**, a neo-Gothic brick church just behind the **casino**.

FRÉJUS

This pleasant town just off the sea was founded by the Romans. The old settlement lies on a small hill while the new town has evolved around a smart marina.

Roman Fréjus ★★★

A legacy of the Romans, the *arènes*, or amphitheatre (open Wednesday to Monday, morning and afternoon), was built in the 1st century AD and could hold up to 10,000 spectators for its gladiatorial combats and deadly

confrontations with wild animals. The subterranean maze of central corridors, in crucifix form, are what is left of the passageways that were used by man, beast, machinery and decor – all part of the show.

Another building made for spectators was the **theatre**, probably built around the same time as the amphitheatre. Its stage and the supports for the raked seating are still clearly visible.

More Roman remains in the form of an **aqueduct** lie just outside the city. Approximately 40km (25 miles) of watercourse, supported often by arches and bridges, was constructed to supply Roman Fréjus with water. There are also some Roman **city walls** punctuated by semi-circular **towers** (clos de la Tour) which delineate the extent of the original town.

Fréjus also has a good **Musée Archéologique Municipal** (place Calvini, open from Monday to Saturday, morning and afternoon), where you'll come face to face with a Roman head of Jupiter, an unusual mosaic leopard and the twin-headed Hermès, symbol of the town of Fréjus.

Cathédrale Saint-Léonce ***

Dating back to the 11th century, the cathedral boasts two interesting pieces of architecture. The first is a 5th-century baptistry, which can be viewed from the exterior.

The second, and highlight of the cathedral complex is, without a doubt, the **Cloître**, one of the prettiest cloisters in the south of France. The arches are held aloft by pencil-thin columns and simple carved capitals. But it is the marvellous **wooden ceiling**, a superb example of carpentry, which complements the play of light and shade. And, within the beams and partitions are painted plaques of small figures which date from the 14th century.

Les Arcs *

Wine and a well-conserved medieval quarter draw most visitors to Les Arcs. **Le Parage**, as the old part of town is known, is a small but fascinating area of tiny paved alleys dominated by the Château de Villeneuve. For the less historically inclined it is the wines under the label **Côtes de Provence** that bring them here, for the town is a centre of wine production. A visit to the nearby **Maison des Vins** (on the national road N7) is an interesting experience to taste and learn about the different wines grown in this *appellation contrôlée*.

Above: *The 11th-century cloisters in the cathedral of Saint-Léonce in Fréjus.*
Opposite: *A sculpture of Hermès, a legacy of the Roman era in Fréjus.*

LES CÔTES DE PROVENCE

Over 100 million bottles contribute to making the Côtes de Provence the sixth largest wine-producing region in France. Its *appelation* was not always highly appreciated, but in the last decade modern technology and increasing interest in winemaking has considerably improved the quality of its wines. Some 75 per cent of these are rosé and 20 per cent are red, but local œnologues are increasingly producing quality white wines from grapes such as Rolle, Sémillon, Clairette and Ugni-blanc.

Right: *Le Parage is the medieval area of the old town of les Arcs.*

If you drive towards Salernes from les Arcs, you'll pass the town of **Lorgues**, noted for its medieval towers and some fine 18th-century municipal architecture. The road northwards from Lorgues heads towards the beautiful **Lac de Sainte-Croix** (*see* page 73) via either the town of Salernes or **Villecroze** (noted for its troglodyte homes).

Le Thoronet ★★

The importance of this small village lies in the abbey which takes its name, approximately 8km (5 miles) further on up the Argens valley. The **Abbaye du Thoronet** is located deep in the wooden hills of the Darboussière Forest – a wonderfully bucolic setting, ideal for meditation. Founded in the mid-12th century, it was the first Cistercian building in France and, along with Sénanque (*see* page 65) and Silvacane (*see* page 41), is the third of the great Cistercian abbeys in Provence. It is a fine example of Provençal Romanesque architecture. Its ancient dry stones – each laid without mortar – breathe tranquillity and strength and nowhere more so than in the beautiful **cloisters**, constructed on single columns. To one side is the **hexagonal lavabo**, used for drinking and for ablutions prior to eating in the **refectory** (there are only traces left today). The **Chapter House**, where a chapter from Saint Benedict's rule would be read daily,

TROUBADOURS

Provençal poets of the 12th to 14th centuries wrote lyric poetry that was to have a profound influence on the subject and form of European verse. The troubadours were famous for *cansos*, ballads that introduced the concept of and endorsed courtly love. They were also noted for *sirventes*, satires on politics and war. Their name derives from the old Provençal verb *trobar* (to find or invent). Their works were often performed by minstrels who wandered from castle to castle and a number of troubadours were enthusiastically patronized by European courts.

is in fine form and rather more decorated than other areas. The abbey also has an interesting **cellar room** in which the monks used to make wine and olive oil (their primary source of income) and there are still some 18th-century wine vats, and a few of their tools on display.

Saint-Maximin-la-Sainte-Baume ★★★

The huge basilica **Sainte-Marie-Madaleine** dominates the valley through which the A8 motorway, *La Provençale*, slices and provides a focal point as you drive through Saint-Maximin towards the building. Crossing the place de l'Hôtel de Ville, where the town hall's handsome façade is somewhat overshadowed by the basilica's unfinished western entrance, you enter into the vast basilica. Behind you stands the impressively large **organ**, made over 225 years ago. Ahead is the 15th-century wooden retable, known as the **Ronzen's Retable**, while in the middle of the north aisle a flight of stairs leads to the crypt below in which the tomb and skull of **Saint Mary Magdalene** are held. The basilica is believed to have been built on the site of her tomb, alongside that of Saint Cedonius and Saint Maximin (the first bishop of Aix). The magnificently carved stone sacophagi of Saint Cedonius and the mutilated one of Saint Mary date back to the 4th century.

A door leads from the basilica to the large **cloisters** which now house a fine restaurant and exhibition space.

In the nearby Massif de la Sainte-Baume is the cave in which Mary Magdalene is reputed to have spent the last 33 years of her life. This is a favourite place for pilgrims and hikers to visit.

Barjols, north of Saint-Maximin, is noted for its artisans, among them the makers of traditional musical instruments.

> **CHAPELLE SAINTE-ROSELINE**
>
> A couple of kilometres from les Arcs the **Chapelle Sainte-Roseline** is visited for two different reasons. It contains the extraordinarily well-preserved body of the 670-year-old saint (which is on display in a glass cabinet) as well as the enchanting mosaic, *Le Repas des Anges*, created by **Marc Chagall**. Next to the Chapelle, in part of the old **Château Sainte-Roseline**, is an interesting winery whose wines, named for Sainte-Roseline, carry the *Cru Classé* label identifying their high quality.

Below: *Carved detail on the massive doors of Saint-Maximin-La-Sainte-Baume.*

Le Var at a Glance

The summer months are the most popular, but the *arrière saison* – September and October – as well as late spring and early summer are also delightful times to visit. Many of the restaurants and hotels are closed out of season. Check before leaving.

Saint-Tropez is just over 100km (63 miles) from Nice and 136km (85 miles) from Marseille. It is 874km (545 miles) from Paris. The French *autoroute* (motorway) system does not pass along the Var coast. From Marseille the A50 passes by Toulon then veers northeastwards where it joins the A8 (Aix to Nice), continuing on to near Fréjus and Nice. The coast is accessible either by a coastal route (not particularly fast, especially in summer) or by southbound roads from the motorway cutting through the hills and dropping down to the coastal resorts.
The nearest **international airport** is either **Nice-Côte d'Azur** (for information tel: 04 93 21 30 12) or **Marseille Marignane** (for information tel: 04 42 78 21 00), though there is a small domestic airport at **Toulon–Hyères** (for information tel: 04 90 00 83 83) with flights to and from Paris.
The main **railway** route passes from Marseille through

Toulon, via St-Raphaël to Nice and the Italian border. There are regular services and overnight trains to either Italy or Paris. There are no trains which serve the section of the coast between Toulon and Saint-Raphaël.

Car hire is usually the easiest option. The main towns have **intercity buses** and although the services are not frequent inland, the coastal routes are well maintained. For information check with **Sodetrave**, tel: 04 94 95 24 82. Trains are not practical for getting around the Var. There are some seasonal **maritime services** between Saint-Tropez and Cannes, Port-Grimaud and Sainte-Maxime. Check with Transports Maritimes, MMG in Sainte-Maxime, tel: 04 94 96 51 00.

LUXURY
Byblos, av Paul Signac, Saint-Tropez, tel: 04 94 56 68 00, fax: 94 56 68 02, e-mail: saint-tropez@byblos.com
The best address for spotting the rich and famous. Just a few minutes' walk away from the port.
La Ponche, place Révelin, port de pêche, Saint-Tropez, tel: 04 94 97 02 53, fax: 94 97 78 61, e-mail: hotel@laponche.com
Beautiful small hotel, quiet square. Seafront rooms are

the best, but expensive. Moderate low-season tariffs. Good terrace restaurant.
Mas du Langoustier, Ile de Porquerolles, tel: 04 94 58 30 09, fax: 94 58 36 02, e-mail: langoustier@compuserve.com
Open summer only, a delightful hotel in a tranquil island setting on the Iles d'Hyères. Good restaurant.
La Ferme d'Augustin, plage de Tahiti, St-Tropez, tel: 04 94 55 97 00, fax: 94 97 40 30, e-mail: vallet.ferme.augustin @wanadoo.fr
Provençal atmosphere near beaches. Some rooms fall into the mid-range category.
L'Ile Rousse, bd L Lumière, Bandol, tel: 04 94 29 33 00, fax: 94 29 49 49. Good position overlooking bay of Bandol. Fine restaurants.

MID-RANGE
Hôtel Corniche, 17 littoral F Mistral, Morillon, Toulon, tel: 04 94 41 35 12, fax: 94 41 24 58. Small hotel with fine seaside location just 5 minutes from the centre of Toulon.
Auberge de la Calanque, 62 av Gén de Gaulle, le Lavandou, tel: 04 94 71 05 96, fax: 94 71 20 12. An older style hotel with great sea views.

BUDGET
Hôtel Cecil, 17 rue Bonnard, Juan-les-Pins, tel: 04 93 61 05 12, fax: 04 93 67 09 14. Small, family-run hotel in downtown Juan-les-Pins, just a minute from the beach.

Le Var at a Glance

Le Flore, 35 rue Grisolle, Fréjus, tel: 04 94 51 38 35. A very inexpensive and central hotel, 5 minutes from the cathedral.

Hostellerie de l'Abbaye, chemin du Château, Le Thoronet, tel: 04 94 73 88 81, fax: 94 73 89 24. Smallish hotel with pool and restaurant. Well-placed for central Var.

Les Arcades de St-Pons, route du Plan de la Tour, St-Pons les Mûres, (near Port-Grimaud), tel: 04 94 56 38 24, fax: 94 56 36 75. Small hotel, with a friendly atmosphere, well-placed for coast and hinterland.

Hôtel Lou Castellas, route des Moulins de Paillas, Ramatuelle, tel/fax: 04 94 79 20 67. Small, family hotel in Ramatuelle, just 5 minutes from St-Tropez. Good hillside location, excellent, pricey restaurant. Superb views.

Hostellerie Provençale, Ile de Port-Cros, tel: 04 94 05 90 43, fax: 04 94 05 92 90. Right on the port, great location. Restaurant open summer only.

WHERE TO EAT

LUXURY

Port-Royal, pl Tambourinaire, Port-Fréjus, tel: 04 94 53 09 11. Excellent seafood and, in summer, open-air dining.

Leï Mouscardins, near Tour du Portalet, St-Tropez, tel: 04 94 97 29 00. Just behind the port, good for people watching and seafood at one of the village's favourite restaurants.

MID-RANGE

Le Sud, av des 3 Dauphins, Le Lavandou, tel: 04 94 05 76 98. A lovely rustic ambience, excellent food and attentive service make this a good choice.

Petit Charron, 6 rue Charron, St-Tropez, tel: 04 94 97 73 78. A delightful small restaurant behind the port, offering mainly lunches. Booking essential.

L'Aréna, Hôtel L'Aréna, 145 bd Gén de Gaulle, Fréjus, tel: 04 94 17 09 40. Excellent value, regional cuisine. Also a moderately priced hotel.

L'Écurie, Hôtel Lou Castellas (see Where to Stay). Spectacular terrace dining with innovative Provençal cuisine.

BUDGET

Relais de la Poste, place Poste, Sanary-sur-Mer, tel: 04 94 74 22 20. In the old part of town, a good address. Affordable, and with gourmet menus.

L'Auberge Provençale, 11 rue Patron Ravello, le Lavandou, tel: 04 94 71 00 44, fax: 04 94 15 02 25, e-mail: provençale.auberge@ wanadoo.fr Charming small restaurant in equally appealing small hotel.

Chez Mimi, 83 av de la Republique, Toulon, tel: 04 94 92 79 60. A typical Tunisian restaurant on the edge of the old town. Inexpensive.

SHOPPING

The area is not particularly known for any specific products. Bandol, part of the AOC Provence wines, produces good wine. Shopping in the coastal resorts is usually for luxury clothes, jewellery and accessories. Top of the list has to be St-Tropez with some excellent shops. This is definitely the place to indulge in luxury beachwear and suitable bijoux.

USEFUL CONTACTS

Office de tourisme, place J-Raimu, Toulon, tel: 04 94 18 53 00.

Office de tourisme, quai G-Péri, le Lavandou, tel: 04 94 71 05 96.

Office de tourisme, quai J-Jaurès, St-Tropez, tel: 04 94 97 45 21.

Office de tourisme, rue J-Jaurès, Fréjus, tel: 04 94 51 83 83.

Office de tourisme, Rotonde j-Salusse, av Belgique, Hyères, tel: 04 94 65 18 55.

Aloha, le Lavandou, tel: 04 94 05 67 06. Sailing trips out to the Iles d'Hyères.

La Maison des Vins, route nationale 7, Les Arc-sur-Agens, tel: 04 94 47 48 47. A good place to get to grips with the wines from La Côte de Provence. Tasting and sales.

Travel Tips

Tourist Information

The French Government Tourist Office has branches overseas that can offer detailed information and maps. They are to be found in **London** (178 Piccadilly, London W1V OA, tel: 0891 824-4123, fax: 020 7493-6594); **New York** (444 Madison Ave, NY10022, tel: 212 838-7800, fax: 212 838-7855); **Montreal** (1981 Avenue McGill College, Suite 490, Que H3A2W9, tel: 514 845-4868); **Sydney** (BNP Building, 12th floor, 12 Castlereagh St, Sydney, NSW 2000, tel: 02 231-5244, fax: 02 221-8682) and **Cape Town** (Pinnacle Building, cnr Burg and Castle St, Cape Town, 8000, tel: 21 462-4260, fax: 21 462-4266). Provence and the Côte d'Azur are listed in many instances on the Internet and much useful information can be gleaned from this source: www.provencetourism.com or www.provenceweb.fr Each town in France has its *Syndicat d'Initiative* or an *Office de Tourisme* with a wealth of information.

Entry Requirements

EU citizens require either a valid, full passport or an identity card to visit France. Other nationalities may enter with a valid passport. Visitors from Australia, New Zealand and South Africa require a visa. All visitors may stay a maximum of 90 days, after which a resident's permit is required.

Customs

There is no duty-free allowance between France and EU countries. Visitors coming from Switzerland and other European (including Andorra) or overseas countries may import one litre of spirits, two litres of wine and 200 cigarettes without incurring duty.

Health Requirements

There are no specific health requirements to enter France. However, some precautions and home remedies are worth considering (*see* Health Precautions on page 125).

Getting there

Provence is easily accessible by plane, train and car.

By Air: Nice-Côte d'Azur (for information tel: 04 93 21 30 12), the region's largest international airport, is just 7km (4.5 miles) from the city and receives flights from all parts of Europe (including frequent daily flights on Air France, British Airways, Easyjet and British Midland from Great Britain), a few flights from North America, as well as frequent flights from Paris. Travellers coming to the region from other continents will have to transfer in Paris and may also have to change airports. Try to arrive and depart from Paris' **Charles de Gaulle** to avoid having to change airports and possible delays. The region's second airport, **Marseille Marignane** (for information tel: 04 42 78 21 00) is located 28km (22.5 miles) west of Marseille and is also a growing airport with many international flights and connections with the capital. The Aéroport de **Nîmes-Arles-Camargue** is located conveniently 8km (5 miles) south of Nîmes on the road to Arles. For information, tel: 04 66 70 06 88. Daily Ryanair flights from London Stansted. Avignon and Toulon also have airports with connections to Paris, though in the case of the latter it is quicker to take the high-speed train.

For those visitors requiring greater mobility at their destination, a number of competitive fly-drive packages exist. Enquire about these back home as they are usually far cheaper when pre-paid.

By Rail: France's high-speed TGV (*Train à Grande Vitesse*) train network is continuously extending and will eventually take in Nice, making a fast connection with Avignon, Lyons and Paris in the north. The newest section (Paris–Marseille) takes just three hours. There are also intercity connections between the north and south. Menton, Nice and Marseille are all on the Italy-Spain intercity route which travels onward through Montpellier to Barcelona.

By Road: Provence and the Côte d'Azur are connected to the rest of France and to Italy by a series of toll-paying *autoroutes*, free *routes nationales* and the smaller country *routes départementales*. The busy **A7 motorway**, dubbed the *Autoroute du Soleil*, links Paris with Marseille. It becomes the A50 as it continues towards Toulon, and the A57 as it continues northwards. The A8-E80 links Aix-en-Provence with Nice and the Italian border.

Airport tax: Airport tax is not collected at French airports as it is included in the price of an air ticket.

What to Pack

Light clothes for the **summer** months (with a woollen jacket for the evenings and, perhaps, a rainproof jacket for visits to the mountains) and warmer clothes for **winter**. The temperatures in midwinter definitely require a coat or jacket, though on the coast one can sometimes sit out in shirt sleeves at midday. Restaurants on the Riviera are generally trendy rather than formal, but the smarter addresses will expect decorous dress and ties. Elsewhere, casual dressing is now the norm. Skiing gear can be rented at the larger resorts, though it is probably better to bring your own ski jacket and salopettes so as not to be disappointed.

Money Matters

Currency: As of 2002, the Euro is the official currency. It's usually worth 6.56 French Francs but its conversion rate fluctuates against the British Pound and the American Dollar. There are 8 coins (1, 2, 5, 10, 20 and 50 cents, and 1 and 2 Euros) and 7 denominations (5, 10, 20, 50, 100, 200 and 500 Euros) of paper money. These are all legal tender in all 12 countries in the Euro Zone.

Banks: They are generally open from 08:00 to noon, and again 14:00–17:00, Monday–Friday. Most people, however, use the ATM system, or *distributeur automatique* as the French call them, to get cash rather than using the slower banking services.

These **ATMs** accept most credit cards, VISA and Mastercard being the most popular. France is moving increasingly towards a cash-less society. For payment of hotel, restaurant, petrol bills and most shopping over 15 Euros in value, a VISA or Mastercard is indispensible.

Accommodation

There are several options from luxurious palaces to simple rooms in family-run hotels. Towns have a fine choice of accommodation but there are also many rural hotels with considerable character that should be considered. Often the best hotels also have renowned restaurants. In the low season, expect to pay over 140 Euros (830F) for a double room in a luxury hotel (and considerably more for a luxury room in season on the Côte d'Azur); 80-140 Euros (500-830F) for a double room in a mid-range hotel; and less than 75 Euros (460F) for a room in the budget category. During the high season prices rise considerably and tourists are often asked to take half board.

Transport

Air: There are no domestic flights within Provence and the Côte d'Azur but the two most important airports – Nice and Marseille – have regular flights between the capital and the south of France. Air France, AOM, and Air Littorale all operate in this area. Foreign airlines to fly into either Nice or Marseille include British Airways, Easyjet, Air UK and British Midland, while Ryanair serves Nîmes and Marseille. Alternatively, Montpellier is a useful airport for visitors travelling to the western Camargue. Local buses take travellers from the airports to the town centres.

Road: The road system is excellent in France. *Autoroutes* (designated by the letter 'A' before a number) provide the country with toll-paying motorways, the *routes nationales* or national roads (designated by the letters 'RN') link the major towns, while the *routes départementales* connect the smaller towns and are designated by the letter 'D'. A detailed map, such as the *Globetrotter Travel Map of Provence and the Côte d'Azur*, is of great benefit for navigation of the towns as well as the surrounding countryside. The **speed limits** in France are 130kph (81mph) on motorways under dry conditions, 110kph (70mph) if it is rainy. On dual-carriage roads the limit is 110kph

(70mph), on other rural roads it is 90kph (56mph), while in urban areas it is 50kph (30mph), occasionally dropping to 30kph (20mph) in areas with lots of pedestrians. French police use radar to check speed and will also randomly stop drivers to check that they have the **correct documents** and to verify their alcohol intake. Seat belts in both front and back of a car are obligatory, as are crash helmets for bikers. On-the-spot fines are commonly issued to offenders.

In France a driver must be able to produce his car's documents, his own identity papers (passport or ID card) and a valid **driving licence** at all times.

For drivers bringing in their own car, a valid *carte verte* (**green card**) is necessary to prove that the car is properly insured. A red emergency triangle is also required in case of a breakdown. Note that, unless clearly indicated otherwise, cars arriving from the right always have priority. Cars can be **hired** at all the airports in major cities. Hertz,

Avis, Europcar and ADA are all popular. Package prices offering a rental car in conjunction with an air ticket or train fare are often far better deals than on-the-spot rentals.

Buses: There is an adequate system of buses linking the major towns in the area. It is probably wiser to check with the local tourist offices to ensure good connections. Some of the smaller villages have infrequent services to and from the larger towns.

Train: The *Société Nationale de Chemins de Fer*, **SNCF**, operates trains in France. The fast *Train à Grande Vitesse* (TGV) service from Paris now travels as far as Nice, cutting travel time considerably from the capital. The Eurostar services from Britain pass by either Paris or Lille and make travelling by train from London to Provence faster than by car. Other services, such as the **Grande Lignes**, also link towns. Major rail hubs include Avignon, Marseille, Toulon, Saint-Raphaël and Nice. There is no railway line along the coast of Var.

Business Hours

Opening hours are staggered according to the nature of the business. Practically every French establishment, except department stores, closes for lunch.

Government offices are open weekdays only from 08:00–12:00 and usually again from 14:00–17:00.

Post offices, in addition to the above hours, open on Saturday from 09:00–11:30.

CONVERSION CHART		
FROM	**TO**	**MULTIPLY BY**
Millimetres	Inches	0.0394
Metres	Yards	1.0936
Metres	Feet	3.281
Kilometres	Miles	0.6214
Square kilometres	Square miles	0.386
Hectares	Acres	2.471
Litres	Pints	1.760
Kilograms	Pounds	2.205
Tonnes	Tons	0.984
To convert Celsius to Fahrenheit: x 9 ÷ 5 + 32		

Businesses tend to start at 09:00, stop for lunch and open again until 19:00. Small shops (except bakers and greengrocers, who often open much earlier) open around 9:30 or 10:00, closing for lunch and re-opening at either 14:00 in winter, or 15:00 in summer, until 19:00 or 20:00.

Banks open weekdays at 08:00, closing just before 12:00 and reopening from 14:00–17:00. Some banks (especially in the very popular tourist resorts) operate on Saturday mornings.

Museum opening hours are somewhat different. They are usually open for longer during the summer months (June to September, inclusive). Most are open five to six days a week, 09:00 to noon, and 14:00 or 15:00–19:00. In this guide we have used the term, 'morning and afternoon' to note that the establishment closes at lunchtime.

Time Difference

France is on Central European Time. In winter this is GMT plus one hour and in summer, GMT plus two hours. Thus in winter when it is 12 noon in London, it is 13:00 in Nice. In summer, clocks are put forward an hour.

Communications

The international telephone dialling code for France is 33. All the numbers in Provence and the Côte d'Azur start with an '04' which needs to be dialled even from within the country. When calling from another country, however, the '0' is dropped. To call overseas from France, dial '00' followed by the country and town code. Post offices, stations and tobac-conists sell telephone cards, cartes téléphoniques, to call both locally and overseas. In airports you can use a VISA, Mastercard or other credit card to make long-distance calls. Home Country Direct also works from France. Check with your home operator (British Telecom or similar) for the correct access numbers. The postal services in and from France are reliable and fairly fast. Post offices are open from 09:00–12:00 and from 14:00–17:00. Stamps are also available from tabacs. The cost of sending a letter or card from France is the same as anywhere in the EC.

Electricity

The voltage in France is 220 volts. Plugs are two-pin, either round or flat. An adapter is necessary for British, Australian and South African plugs, while 110 volt appliances made in the USA will be irreparably damaged in Europe.

Health Precautions

There appear to be very few health risks in the south of France these days. The water in hotel and restaurant taps must legally be potable, and it is often very good although the fashion for mineral water, which started with Vichy water and now covers several different kinds, is still rising.

USEFUL PHRASES

Bonjour • Good day

Bonsoir • Good evening

Au revoir • Goodbye

Merci bien •
Thanks very much

Excusez-moi • Excuse me

Comment allez-vous? •
How are you?

Très bien, merci •
Very well, thank you

Oui/non • Yes/no

S'il vous plaît...(written as svp) • Please

Je vous en prie • You are welcome/don't mention it

Au secours! • Help!

Arrêtez! • Stop!

Parlez-vous anglais? •
Do you speak English?

Je ne comprends pas •
I don't understand

Quel est le prix de... •
How much does ... cost?

C'est trop cher •
It's too expensive

A quelle heure on ferme? •
When do you close?

Où est l'hôtel X, svp? •
Where's the Hotel X, please?

Faites le plein, svp •
Fill up the tank please

Péage • Toll (on motorway)

A gauche/droite •
Turn left/right

Tout droit • Straight ahead

À quelle heure part le train pour X? • What time does the train for X leave?

Avez-vous une chambre double/simple pour la nuit? •
Do you have a double/single room for the night?

La carte, svp •
The menu please

Une pression • Draft beer

Un verre de vin blanc/rouge/rosé • A glass of white/red/rosé wine

Eau minerale, gazeuse/plate • Mineral water, fizzy/still

The main health hazards are sunburn, the odd insect bite and perhaps, for snorkellers who inadvertently brush with a sea urchin, spines in a limb. Take care in the sun and not only cover up with a hat but use a high-factor (SPF) sun protection cream. The French still enjoy sunning topless but they are learning to use high-factor protection. Unfortunately, premature skin ageing and sun cancer are a big risk for habitués of the Riviera. Mosquitoes and midges are common around the lakes and rivers (especially in the Haute-Provence area) so come armed with a good repellent. If you suffer from diarrhoea for longer than 24 hours, consult a pharmacy or doctor. Pharmacies can provide off-the-shelf remedies and advice. Major medical problems or accidents can be treated at the local hospitals. The medical services in France are good and relatively inexpensive. EU members may be entitled to free emergency treatment if they have brought with them an E111 form obtainable from a post office in their EU home town. **Health insurance** is always advisable when travelling, and one which includes emergency evacuation is a good idea.

Personal Safety

Safeguarding France's law and order is the job two departments – the **police** (a service that takes care of the community as well as dealing with minor infrac-

tions) and the **gendarmerie**, a law-enforcement organization with a military hierarchy (which deals with more serious crimes).

France is generally a safe country. The usual advice about not walking alone at night or carrying big flashy cameras in public places is always worth considering. There is some trouble with car theft and breaking into cars, especially on the Riviera. The rule of thumb here is never to leave anything that could tempt a break-in, such as a handbag or expensive sunglasses, in your vehicle. If you break down on a motorway or dual carriageway, lock the car and walk to the nearest emergency telephone. They are spaced every 2km (just over a mile) or so apart along all major roads.

Emergencies

For accident assistance dial **15** to get help from the SAMU (*Service d'assistance médicale d'urgence*). For police emergencies dial **17** to speak to the local police or gendarmerie. In case of a fire dial **18** to contact the *Sapeurs Pompiers*.

Etiquette

The French appreciate good manners. A *bonjour* on entering a shop, an *au revoir* on leaving and a frequent *merci* to thank people for services is appropriate. The French shake hands when they meet new people, but greetings between friends take the form of cheek kissing – two to four, depending on where they come from! Clothing etiquette seems nonexistent: shorts, T-shirts and tiny skirts hardly raise an eyebrow, except in churches where a level of decorum is expected. Beachwear is minimal and usually topless. Nude bathing is tolerated in certain areas (such as near Saint-Tropez).

Tipping

This is still a thorny subject. The French are not great tippers and their American cousins make them look mean. At a bistro or café it is customary to round up the bill. In some of the smarter restaurants, a 'voluntary' service charge of around 10 per cent is often included. If the service was very poor, you can decline to pay it.

Good Reading

Bogarde, **Dirk** (1988) *A Postillion Struck by Lightning*, (1990) *A Gentle Occupation*, (1992) *Voices in the Garden*, Penguin.
Durrell, **Lawrence** (1994) *Provence*, Arcade.
Fortescue, **Lady** (reprinted 2000) *Perfume from Provence*, Black Swan.
Jones, **Louïsa** (1992) *Gardens in Provence*, Flammarion.
Mayle, **Peter** (1994) *Hôtel Pastis*, (reprinted 2000) *A Year in Provence*, (reprinted 2000) *Encore Provence*, (1998) *Chasing Cézanne*, Pan.
Saint-Exupéry, **Antoine** (2000) *The Little Prince*, translated by Richard Howard, Mammoth.
Suskind, **Patrick** (1989) *Perfume*, Penguin.

INDEX

Note: Numbers in **bold** indicate photographs